THE MOON RISES IN EMPTY SPACE

THE MOON RISES IN EMPTY SPACE

Commentaries on the Il-Won-Sang Vow

Venerable Kyongsan

The Moon Rises In Empty Space

Published by Won Dharma Publications
361 Route 23, Claverack, NY 12513, USA
Phone: 518-851-2581

Library of Congress Control Number: 2022917633
ISBN: 979-8-9869466-0-3

Cover design by Kathy Abeyatunage

Printed in the Republic of Korea

CONTENTS

PREFACE

LEADING THE WAY INTO AN IL-WON WORLD

With an Empty Mind

"The act of applying colors takes place after the surface has been cleaned," Confucius says, in the *Analects*—we first prepare the canvas and only then we begin to paint. Before we make rice, we first wash the bowl and we rinse the grains. When we invite guests to our home, we clean before they arrive, and we wash our hands before we prepare the food. In the same way, it is important that we empty our mind before we put it to use.

No matter how hard the rain beats down, the beads of water roll off the lotus leaf. If we can restore the pristine nature of our original mind, the sensory conditions we face will roll off much as the rain trickles down the lotus leaf. Let us then make sure to establish a clean and pure mind before we begin any new activity. In preparation for this lecture on the Il-Won-Sang Vow, I emptied my mind and committed to fully maintaining an open heart. I encourage all of you who are listening to this lecture to approach it having first cleared your mind, so you can receive far greater benefits.

A GREAT EVENT

There have been many events in the history of humankind that call for celebration. Thomas Edison's discovery of electric power generation and his invention of the electric light bulb were great events. The end of the First and Second World Wars, the fall of the Berlin Wall, the day Yuri Gagarin traveled outside the earth's atmosphere on the world's first space voyage, and the day Neil Armstrong set foot on the moon were great causes for celebration.

But these were external events of a cultural nature. There have been even greater causes for celebration. Great sages appeared on the horizon of human history like the rising of the sun and the moon. When the Buddha came to this world three thousand years ago, it was a truly great event. So were the arrivals of Confucius and Jesus Christ.

There was another great, if lesser known, event in human history. In 1916 C.E., the Founding Master Sotaesan achieved great enlightenment. That year marks the first year of the Won Buddhist Era. Much of humanity is still unaware of this event. But as we help open the eyes of many, the Founding Master's arrival on this Earth becomes an even greater cause for celebration as well as a source of wisdom.

In the past, when a sage came to this world, the impact of that event was limited to the region surrounding the sage's birthplace. The arrival of Confucius was a great event principally for China, the arrival of Jesus Christ for Judea and the arrival of the Buddha for India.

These great sages of the past came to affect only one of the cardinal directions. Even though they are certain to continue to have as great an impact on the spiritual civilization of humanity in the future as they do today, it took significantly long periods of time—many centuries—for them to become known to the rest of the world.

The Founding Master came to this world at the dawning of a globalized era to be a teacher for all directions—north, south, east, and west. He was therefore able to address the issues of the contemporary world as a unity. It will be a great day when the whole world awakens to his teachings.

Today we live in an age of human achievements in which we can change our destinies. For that reason, what people realize or do during their lives is far more important than the date of their births. In the past, it was significantly more difficult for people to change the destinies into which they had been born, so it was customary to celebrate the lives of sages on their birthdays.

The Founding Master placed great value on the day of his enlightenment, so that is the date when Won Buddhism celebrates the Founding Master's life and work.

In the future, external conditions will be of little importance. Instead, it will be a time in which we will evaluate if a person awakened to the Truth while living in this world, as well as what benefits that person brought to the world. What family a person was born into, whether that person was a man or woman, his or her race, or birth date will have little importance.

It is important that Won Buddhists approach these lectures on the Il-Won-Sang Vow as a way to gain understanding of their own minds, to awaken to the Truth of the universe and to come to terms with what they will choose to do while they live in this world.

THE MEANING OF THE FOUNDING MASTER'S ARRIVAL

Why did the Founding Master come to this world? He did not come to tell us, "Believe in my doctrine." Rather, he came to make sages out of all of us.

During the March 1st Movement for the Korean Independence, the Founding Master heard the calls of students asking him to take part in the campaign. He called this event a "Funeral Chant Demanding a Great Opening," for it marked the end of an era. To further the Great Opening, Sotaesan went to Mt. Byeon and wrote down his teachings. "One must not stop at catching fish with a pole," he said at the time, "One must weave a net."

When he began the work of recording his doctrine and creating a plan of action, the Founding Master said that while the March 1 Movement and its goal of saving the Korean people were important, it was more urgent still to provide the world with a new set of principles suited for the future that could save both the Korean people and humanity as a whole.

We now find ourselves caught in and supported by the net crafted by the Founding Master. It is a net that pulls us toward a paradisiacal world—Il-Won world. Now that we are caught, we should not seek to extricate ourselves. Rather, we should allow ourselves to be taken where it leads us, towards building that paradisiacal world. We should remain with this dharma throughout numerous lifetimes, and—while in this present lifetime—change the nameplate above our door. When our descendants write their genealogies, they will describe us not as "average person so and so," but as "sage so and so"—someone possessing the Status of Dharma Strong and Māra Defeated, the Status of Beyond the Household or the Status of Tathāgata.

Usually, we live our lives without understanding this world or the world to come, with no Birth and Death insurance to prepare us for the possibility of misfortune striking us during our lives. For that reason, it is important to make sure our nameplate reads "sage." I pray that you will study the Il-Won-Sang Vow so that you, too, can change your nameplate to "sage" and play a major role in the building of Il-Won world.

Translators' Foreword

It is said that when we get lost in a forest we need to retrace our steps to the last place we recognize as the correct path. Only from there can we proceed with confidence

It is the same when our life and practice are guided by scriptures because they too can lead us astray if we do not understand them correctly.

The most profound of the sacred teachings escape the realm of language. It took extraordinary care from our great teacher, Sotaesan, the founding master of Won Buddhism to create the Il-Won-Sang Vow. It is intricately and exquisitely crafted to contain the essence of the ultimate reality as well as the essential teachings of Won Buddhism.

Translating sutras and books on the dharma is one of the best ways to delve into the deepest meaning of the teachings and their original intention. Having to find just the correct word, term or phrase to convey what the text is saying, having to explore the many possibilities of its meaning, is a challenging adventure along the search for Truth.

The Il-Won-Sang Vow is the Heart Sutra of Won Buddhism. Its study and understanding are crucial to Won Buddhists. Sotaesan said that even if the world as we know it were to cease to exist, the Il-Won-Sang Vow would make it possible for Won Buddhism to be revived again.

It is therefore, greatly auspicious that Ven. Kyongsan, the Fourth Head Dharma Master of Won Buddhism, wrote these commentaries on the Il-Won-Sang Vow, which were previously published under the title, *The Moon of the Mind Rises in Empty Space*. (Seoul Selection, 2011)

Since the book had been well received in America, last year we embarked on a reworking of the existing translation of that edition to make it more accessible to practitioners at all levels. Soon we began to find areas of the translation that, when it came to the profound meanings, were unclear. We went back to the original Korean text—the point from which we knew we could reclaim the true meanings. It then became clear that we needed to embark on a new English translation that would consider the current usages of the English language within the context of this millennium.

One of the most fascinating aspects of this creative process was how the true substance of the teachings in this fundamental sutra came to the surface once the more extraneous misnomers were deleted or changed. The third pass of corrections for the new manuscript was transformational. There are so many layers of teachings in this text that the true image of the foundational doctrine and its sound practice become clear only after several readings. That is why Master Kyongsan, when writing these commentaries on the Il-Won-Sang Vow, suggested we chant it thousands or millions of times. Chanting and reading it will not just guide us in our practice, it will give rise to the commitment, in our minds and hearts, to make a great vow to become one with Il-Won-Truth.

Practice based on the multiple readings of this text begins to take shape on its own, without the usual resistance we encounter when on a quest to incorporate new teachings into our practice, or when we aim to change our long-held habits. Instead, it seems to take shape effortlessly because it becomes engrained in our minds.

The basic purpose of this new translation is to motivate practitioners to contemplate and put into practice Sotaesan's intention—that the practice of buddhadharma should be useful to enrich their spiritual practice as well as their daily lives.

In previous translations of the Won Buddhist Scriptures, there are different English terms used for the same concepts in both the doctrine and the practice. A great effort was made in this new translation to consolidate those terms and set a standard for future translations and for the spreading of the dharma to all. To achieve the latter purpose, the translation of the Il-Won-Sang Vow itself was revised to ensure faithfulness to Sotaesan's foundational and deepest teachings.

We sincerely hope and pray that practitioners all around the world will give rise to a great vow of their own, for the benefit of all beings.

ACKNOWLEDGMENTS: We are sincerely and humbly grateful to those who were involved in the translation of the first edition of this book, for their careful rendition; and to Jane Laudi for her insightful corrections in this edition.

NOTE: Regarding proper names and references to teachings and practices, as well as the titles of classic literature, we chose to keep the romanization of Asian terms as they are used in other Won Buddhism books and writings. For example, although Taoism is the term mostly used in the west, we chose Daoism, as it is used in Won Buddhist texts. For Tai Chi, the term 'westerners commonly use, we chose Taiji, which is how we find it in classic Won Buddhist literature.

For clarification we show the term commonly used in the west, in parenthesis, the first few times we use each alternate term.

We hope this is helpful for all readers.

Dosung Yoo and Isabel Barton
Claverack, New York, 2022

THE IL-WON-SANG VOW

Il-Won is the realm of Samādhi beyond words and speech and the gateway of birth and death that transcends being and nonbeing. It is the origin of heaven and earth, parents, fellow beings and laws and the original nature of all buddhas, enlightened masters, unenlightened people, and sentient beings.

Il-Won manifests as both permanence and impermanence.

Viewed as permanence, Il-Won unfolds into an infinite realm that is spontaneous and ever-abiding just as it is.

Viewed as impermanence, Il-Won unfolds into infinite worlds through the cycle of formation, duration, decay and extinction of the universe, and the birth, aging, illness, and death of all beings.

According to how we use our minds and bodies in the four forms of birth as we transform through the six realms of existence, we progress or regress, giving rise to grace from harm, or harm from grace.

Therefore, by modeling ourselves after Il-Won-Sang, the Dharmakāya Buddha, we unawakened beings vow to practice wholeheartedly to cultivate our minds and bodies perfectly; to know human affairs and universal principles perfectly; and to use our minds and bodies perfectly, so we can progress rather than regress and receive grace rather than harm, until we attain the awesome power of Il-Won and become one with the nature of Il-Won.

COMMENTARY ON THE IL-WON-SANG VOW

THE VOW TO BECOME ONE WITH TRUTH

The Il-Won-Sang Vow is a prayer the practitioner offers before the Fourfold Grace of the Dharmakāya Buddha. It is a pledge to attain buddhahood and deliver all sentient beings to the ultimate bliss of Nirvana by becoming one with the perfect, complete substance and nature of Il-Won-Sang Truth. As a result, the practitioner making the vow will forever receive limitless grace from the utterly unbiased and selfless power of Il-Won-Sang Truth.

Master Daesan described the Il-Won-Sang Vow as a pledge offered before one's buddha nature. He said that it was a vow to our buddha nature that we will live a life of Truth.

The vow is designed to be recited out loud, as an invocation or prayer. Before we delve deeply into a its study, let us first consider our own personal vows.

There are different ways to live one's life. Some of us live haphazardly and go whichever way the wind blows, while others live diligently, set goals and work hard to achieve them.

Without goals to achieve, we expend our energies without rhyme or reason and never accrue value before we depart this world.

If we take a good look at those who have succeeded in this world, we will see that all of them have led goal-oriented lives. We too, must deeply consider what our life goal is and to how we determine our vow.

When we have a goal we develop an interest in our objective, and when we develop an interest in something we naturally develop an understanding of it. When we gain an understanding, we can put it into practice, and once we put it into practice, we are able to obtain a result. The person who lacks a goal and a vow is destined, instead, to try just once and when it does not work out, either quit outright or go forwards and backwards, ultimately and consequently meandering through life.

Therein lies the importance of discovering what it is we truly want to do. It is crucial to understand how much more valuable and meaningful it all is when our goal is Truth rather than worldly affairs such as money, honors, or power. When our pursuit is in the material world, even success may deliver us substantial troubles.

One cold snowy winter back when I was administrative director for the Seoul District, I was on a train to Iksan sitting next to an elderly gentleman who was elegantly dressed. We soon engaged in pleasant conversation about various life matters, and so I came to learn about the gentleman's discontent.

"People call me a successful man," he said, but confessed to feeling terribly lonely. He was the president of a small company and was in the process of passing the reins of the company on to his youngest son. His oldest son was a doctor, he explained. He was quite boastful about his children.

He had earned his share of money and honors, yet as he approached the end of life, he said, he realized that he could not avoid that thing called death. He was now set to depart, leaving behind all that he had worked so hard to earn and, he explained, all he could think about was that life was empty. He had come to see the transient nature of life, which as the lyrics of a popular song put it, is a "traveler's path."

What was evident upon observing him was that worldly success cannot enrich our true selves. It is time for all of us to deeply consider the goals we have chosen and to what we are striving to achieve.

A LIFE OF SEEKING TO BECOME ONE WITH TRUTH

The vow to become one with Truth gives us the power to transcend the suffering of samsara, to embody our true self and to command our minds and bodies as we wish. So, let us make the vow to become one with Truth—the new goal of our lives—and to commit all our resources to strengthening that vow.

Each of us must earnestly ask ourselves: What should my vow be? For once we have formulated our vow, we will need no encouragement to practice with fire in our hearts. Such is the importance of making this vow.

The Il-Won-Sang Vow is a declaration to model our lives after Il-Won-Sang. Il-Won-Sang means Truth. Christianity chose the word God as the synonym for Truth; Buddhism chose Dharmakāya Buddha; Daoism, Nature; Confucianism, Wuji; and Sotaesan, the Founding Master, called it Il-Won.

Il-Won Sang Vow is a prayer crafted by the Founding Master himself so that each of us could possess Il-Won-Sang Truth as our own and hold it in the palm of our hand. In writing the Il-Won-Sang Vow, Sotaesan took an interest in the lives of us unawakened beings and exhorted each one of us to make the vow and live our lives accordingly.

It is important to recite the vow over and over, and every now and then, to read it reverentially, relishing and pondering every nuance of the dharma instruction. If we recite it over and over—so that it pierces our brain and heart, our hands and feet—the spirit of the Founding

Master's vow will suffuse our minds and bodies.

THE KIND OF WORLD WE ARE BUILDING

Let us consider what kind of world we have built over the course of our lives, the one we built in the past and the one we are building in the present.

First let us ask ourselves if we have built a world of hatred and love. Hatred and love comprise the life of the unawakened person before approaching his death. What is it that we loved so intensely and hated so intensely during our lives?

Second, let us ask ourselves if we have built a world of ignorance dedicated to the body—doing whatever we wish, eating whatever strikes us as delicious, making ourselves up to look attractive, and dedicating ourselves to all kinds of pleasures. That is the life the unawakened person lives.

Third, have we spent our lives cultivating all manner of pretensions in order to impress others rather than doing what is beneficial for ourselves? Ultimately, we might have abandoned our true selves and lived our lives instead for the sake of others—in which case, what we have accumulated as a result is nothing more than a vein sense of glory or a false image of ourselves. That too is the life of the unawakened person.

Fourth, have we lived a life of objectification, banding together with others to slander, hate or take advantage of others? Have we been self-reliant regarding our livelihoods, or have we hung on to our friends and colleagues, expecting to receive benefit from their career or financial success? Or have we changed the course of our life because of someone else's misfortune?

Let us not live the life of the unawakened person, for it is an endless sequence of hatred and love, of living without rhyme or reason, without any understanding of where we come from or where we are going.

My hope is that this lecture will motivate you to set a goal for your life, so that it will go from the life of the unawakened person—a sequence of hate and love and living blindly—to the life of a buddha.

WHAT WE NEED TO BECOME

The Founding Master believed that when we become one with the Truth we achieve the greatest and most holy life—a life that ensures eternal life. He gave us the Il-Won-Sang Vow so that we might live as one with the Truth and be able to build a world of Truth.

If we trust the Il-Won-Sang Vow, awaken to the Il-Won-Sang Vow, and put the Il-Won-Sang Vow into practice, we will live a life of blessings and complete wisdom. Were he alive today, the Founding Master would be praying that the road opens wide for each person who recites this vow, believes in it, and puts it into practice.

When a novelist publishes a book, he hopes that many people will buy it, read it, and enjoy it. A poet, too, hopes that people will read his poems.

It was the same for the Founding Master in giving us this vow. He hoped and prayed that many of us would read, recite, and practice this sutra, gain the awesome power of Truth, unite with its substance and nature, and forever avoid the path of the unawakened. The Founding Master's students, and all the sages, heavenly beings, and asuras also pray that we fervently recite this dharma instruction from the Founding Master—the Il-Won-Sang Vow—that we believe in it, understand it, practice it, and commend it to others.

When we practice this vow, we share our life with the Founding Master and with all the buddha-bodhisattvas of the three time periods of past, present, and future.

THE WORDS OF PAST SAGES

Many of the scriptures delivered by the sages of the past have lost their luster over time, not because they are not good, but because they have faded over the years and become unsuited to the times. In the *Diamond Sutra*, the Buddha spoke of the Last Epoch, the Saddharma-vipralopa, while Jesus said that when the end came, he would return "as a thief in the night." This meant that when the end time arrived, he would come, unseen, do what was entrusted to him, and depart.

If we travel to Beopju Temple on Mt. Songni, we will see that the Buddha has been enshrined not inside, but outside. This is presumably so that he might greet the Maitreya Buddha who, according to prophecy, will take over from Śākyamuni Buddha when the end times draw near.

The past was a time of one buddha and one thousand bodhisattvas. Yet, the Founding Master predicted the future as an era of the global village, as it is today—he said it would be a time of many living buddhas, one thousand tathāgatas and ten thousand bodhisattvas.

The phrase "ten thousand bodhisattvas" does not literally mean ten thousand people who are bodhisattvas. Rather, it refers to the emergence of a myriad of bodhisattvas pouring forth like sesame seeds. If we also diligently accumulate merit we may enter their ranks. If we have come across this dharma but remain unable to enter within, we are both foolish and lazy.

Anyone can become a buddha-bodhisattva if he makes a vow and diligently accumulates merit. In the world of the past, everything valuable lay in the hands of a limited number of people. Foods such as ginseng and items such as brass chafing dishes were the exclusive possessions of the noblest people. Today, not just goods, but also knowledge is available to most. Anyone can become a buddha-bodhisattva by making a dedication to practice.

BECOMING ONE WITH IL-WON-SANG

The Il-Won-Sang Vow is a sutra that instills in us the need to become one with Il-Won-Sang Truth.

If we do not access this Truth, if we instead set our goals on worldly affairs such as money, honors, or privilege, we may find ourselves dissatisfied with success or we may succumb to wayward delusions. Alternatively, once we are one with Truth, worldly benefits will naturally follow even if we do not pursue them, for all things are contained within Il-Won.

I once listened to the recording of a lecture given by a learned shaman, who was invited to speak by the department of Eastern religions at Wonkwang University.

The speaker talked about a man who had established a prominent university in rural Korea. He had been very rich and had dedicated himself to doing extensive social work—such as establishing orphanages and homes for the elderly. One day the man fell ill and, although he traveled overseas for treatment at a famed hospital, there was no improvement in his condition, so he experienced an early death.

His youngest daughter was a teacher. The speaker said that the man had loved her dearly during his lifetime. After his death, the father appeared to his daughter every night to torment her. "Take my spirit," he would say to her.

The daughter prayed, received counseling from clerics and tried all kinds of methods to rid herself of her father's spirit, to no avail. Finally, she decided to participate in a shamanic ceremony during which she would become a shaman herself, in order to exorcise her father's spirit.

Only by becoming a shaman was she able to come to terms with her father's spirit and appease the torment she was experiencing.

At first, she had even believed her father's spirit to be a demon. But the spirit used her body to earn money to persevere in the work to help orphans and the disabled that he had engaged in during his lifetime.

The father had done many good things for others when he was alive, so why was his spirit not delivered?

Even while he was performing all those good deeds, he was being carried along by fixation and attachment rather than by a mind based in Truth—this became a trap that bound him to an evil destiny.

So, we see that no matter what good deeds we may have done, we will not receive the benefits of grace in our next life if we do not have, as our foundation in this life, a mind that is one with Truth. The first thing we must do, then, is to engage in mind practice.

There is an invisible Truth embedded within the myriad things in Heaven and Earth and in the Dharma Realm of Empty Space.

The enlightened person can see that Truth, but the unenlightened person cannot. The Founding Master awakened to that hidden Truth and named it "Il-Won-Sang."

WHY HE CHOSE THAT NAME

Il (一) means One, meaning "that which is unique and has no other," because Truth is singular.

Won (圓) means circle. This means that while it is one, it contains all things—awesome power, all manner of blessings, and myriad creative transformations.

Sang (相), which means image, indicates that even though all things have form, the Truth has none—It is a reminder that Il Won is just a representation, standing in for Truth.

Once we awaken to the existence of Il-Won-Sang, we make a firm vow to become one with Truth.

Every one of us is, in our original nature, a buddha. We can attain buddhahood if we find the buddha seed inside of us and cultivate it. It is said that when we fervently nurture our vow to become a buddha, the buddhas gather in Tusita Heaven and hold an early sanctification ceremony for us. "With such a vow," they say, "that person is certain to become a buddha."

So how should we nurture our vow? We do it through prayer; and we do it when we attend dharma meetings to exchange opinions with people who possess the same belief and have made the same vow.

At the Won Buddhism temple in Seoul, there are three very large ginkgo trees. Imagine the seeds that grew into these mighty trees. They were very small; yet these tiny seeds grew to become those magnificent trees. Likewise, when we plant the seed of a buddha and nurture it within us, it will grow someday into a mighty buddha.

One of Master Daesan's dharma instructions is the "Verse of the Mind Prayer":

"Everywhere my hand touches, everywhere my feet go, everywhere my voice echoes, everywhere my heart reaches"—with these karmic affinities, let us all attain buddhahood and deliver all sentient beings.

Every time I sing this verse, I strengthen my vow, and my heart grows firmer. Once our vow to become a buddha and deliver all sentient beings has grown solid as a rock, it is said we can avoid all adversity from outside and pass all torment as through crossing a doorway. The person who has the noble and firm vow to become a buddha can overcome any harm within and attain buddhahood.

Part I

IL-WON-SANG
TRUTH

SUMMARY OF IL-WON-SANG TRUTH

When the Founding Master attained great enlightenment on April 28 in the first year of the Won Buddhist Year, he said, "All beings are of a single nature. All dharmas originate from one source. The Truth of the principle of neither arising nor ceasing, and the principle of cause and effect, interact in a perfect, rounded, and complete oneness."

He articulated the relationship between the immutable aspect of Truth and all things in the universe, as well as the way in which that relationship creates, nurtures, and transforms the myriad things in Heaven and Earth as it manifests ever-changing creative transformations. The Il-Won-Sang Vow consists of two main sections, the Truth of Il-Won-Sang, what it is, and the practice of Il-Won-Sang, how we can practice it.

How, ultimately, does Truth exist? Is it present in Heaven? Is it present on Earth? This section speaks to the existential aspect of Truth as well as to its nature and structure.

Looking at the Vow, we can see that the Founding Master explains, in great detail, the nature and structure of Truth, so that we can hold it in our hand. This Truth is something no one can envy us for possessing. A country has only one president, so people fight to occupy that position. But while there is only one Truth, it is a realm that both you and I can hold. There is no need to compete for this position, nor is there any need for envy, just as we do not envy a group of people who are all looking longingly at the moon.

Truth is not limited, no matter how many people possess it. Indeed, it is all the better when it is fully used, when we become one with it.

There is a song that was popular many years ago. The lyrics say, "Who is my beloved? Where can my beloved be found? What could my beloved be doing? I want to meet my beloved." "The Truth of Il-Won-Sang" tells us what Truth looks like, what its nature is, and where it exists.

CHAPTER 1

GENERAL CONTENT OF IL-WON-SANG TRUTH

"Il-Won is the realm of Samādhi beyond words and speech and the gateway of birth and death that transcends being and nonbeing..."

Il-Won Truth speaks of the Samādhi state we enter when we practice Zen, which cannot be expressed in words or language. It is a realm of no arising and no ceasing, which transcends the polarities of "is" or "is not," "good," or "bad."

This passage explains to us what kind of person our beloved is. In other words, it deals with the question of the content of the Truth Buddha that we call Il-Won. It explains that Truth has two aspects: essence (or original nature) and function (or Gateway of Birth and Death). This speaks of the duality of Truth that, while being singular, possesses at the same time both an essential aspect and a functional aspect.

When people have two faces, they succumb to contradiction, but Il-Won-Sang Truth possesses duality without contradiction.

Won Buddhism takes Il-Won-Sang Truth as its central tenet. This means that Won Buddhism has adopted Il-Won-Sang Truth as the foundation of its doctrine. All Won Buddhist practitioners regard Il-Wong-Sang as the object of their faith and adopt it as their standard for practice. It is a very precious dharma instruction in which the Founding Master succinctly explains the content of Truth in two clauses of one complex sentence.

First Clause:
"Il-Won is the realm of Samādhi beyond words and speech..."
The words "Il-Won is the realm of Samādhi beyond words and

speech" mean that it is a realm beyond words and language, so it cannot be explained conceptually; it cannot be imagined in one's mind; it cannot be taught through words. It is a realm of ultimate Nonbeing; a realm of perfect bliss; a realm of utmost good; and a realm that exists before any individual mind, parents, or Heaven and Earth come into being.

In the Daodejing (*Tao Te Ching*), this realm is described with the words, "The Way that can be expressed in words is not the true Way." This means that, if we can explain The Way, it is neither an eternal Way nor an absolute Way. Ultimately, the absolute Way is one that cannot be shaped through language.

In the Daoist scripture, Huangdi Yinfujing, we find the words, "The supremely tranquil Way cannot be marked by calendars." This means that, The Way is a realm that cannot be reduced to calculations. In Christian theology, God is of a realm unknown to us. In our own Dharma of Timeless Zen this type of realm is called the Dharma Realm of Empty Space.

The "realm of Samādhi " refers to the genuine realm we reach when we practice deep meditation, where both subject and object become void, so that there is no "I," no "you," no parents, no Heaven and Earth. It is the state before a separate mind emerges, before we emerge from our parents, before Heaven and Earth are divided. This is the Truth that provides the foundation for Il-Won-Sang Truth—the realm of Samādhi—an absolute oneness that we are incapable of imagining with our ordinary minds.

If we live our lives without knowledge and experience of this realm of Samādhi , we find ourselves constructing ideas and creating more and more thoughts. For example, we might compare our children with the children of others. Or, if a classmate or someone close to us is promoted, we might construct thoughts that trouble our minds with defilements and delusions.

The universal Truth is a place of absolute oneness beyond the division of subjects and objects. It is a state of Samādhi regardless of how things transform—it remains unmoved through the changing of the seasons, from spring to summer to fall to winter. We practitioners can enter a state of Samādhi when our dualistic mind ceases. The Heart Sutra describes the mental functions of sensations, perceptions, volitions, and consciousness. If we merely sense but our mind remains still, we have entered Samādhi. If we recognize the sensation in our mind but we do not react, we are in an early state of Samādhi.

For example, if a car passes by and we hear it but do not perceive it as noisy, that is Samādhi. We can train ourselves to do this—merely listening without thinking—so we can enter Samādhi wherever we happen to be. No matter how noisy and loud a sound may be, if we do not think it is noisy, if we do not label it as loud, it could be said that we are entering a state of Samādhi and that we have taken the first step toward becoming one with Samādhi, the state of Truth.

If we understand the Samādhi state of Truth as the state where there is no "you" or "I," where everything is empty, we understand one half of the Truth. It may be said that we must first travel to this place and back before we can travel to perfect bliss and the kingdom of God.

With God, there are no degrees of kinship. The grandson calls God "father," and the grandfather calls God "father." This is a realm without distinctions of high and low. Master Daesan gave that realm the name of "The Great Equality." In the realm of Truth, the Buddha and all average people and sentient beings are equal.

Only when we know this realm can we understand equality and know what is true. Someone may tell us to be true to ourselves, but if we do not know this realm of Samādhi, we do not know what is true, so we cannot be a true person. This realm is not far away, nor is it difficult to reach. If we let go of a single thought, that is the first step toward Samādhi and the realm of our essential nature.

We create objects of mind to differentiate the many people and phenomena in this world into various categories. But there is only one Il-Won-Sang Truth, so there is nothing to objectify. If there were two Il-Won Truths in this world, we would differentiate each Truth from the other. Since there is but one Truth that dwells in a state of Samādhi as a transcendent entity, past, present, and future are one. We call this realm the Truth that neither arises nor ceases.

Second Clause:
"...and the Gateway of Birth and Death that transcends being and nonbeing..."

Truth is constantly active in its Samādhi state. It creates and nurtures all things from an unbiased position that transcends differentiations of "existing and nonexistent," "good and bad," "right and wrong." The words Birth and Death here mean that Il Won is a Gateway of creative transformations that causes all things to come into being and to return to nonbeing.

Whenever we form a human relationship, we typically approach it with a biased mind—one that views affinity as being present or absent and rushes to either favor or disapprove. Also, we give and take without equality. We give to those we favor and refrain from giving to those we dislike. This biased mind may cause us to love or hate others in the process. It is a common occurrence for sentient beings to fixate on hatred and love and to act from a distorted perspective.

Il-Won-Sang Truth, instead, distributes without bias to all things, from a realm that transcends notions of fondness or loathing.

Gateway of Birth and Death here also mean that we will receive both benefit and harm—which will include when we live and when we die—according to our actions.

I, the one delivering this lecture, have now entered the winter of life. I do not wish to grow older, yet I do find myself growing older and approaching death. If I ask what it is that draws me toward old age and death in this way, I will see that it is none other than Il-Won-Sang Truth. Truth is what pulls me toward old age and death. But Il-Won-Sang Truth does so without bias, from a realm that transcends differentiation between favor and disfavor. This is the Gateway of Birth and Death, and its principle is the karmic principle of cause and effect.

If the realm of Samādhi can be described as the essence—original nature—that neither arises nor ceases, then the Gateway of Birth and Death can be described as the function—or the karmic principle of cause and effect. Il-Won is a combination of these two aspects—the realm of Samādhi beyond words and speech, as well as the Gateway of Birth and Death that transcends Being and Nonbeing. In each of these phrases, the latter part describes the former. "Beyond words and speech" describes "the realm of Samādhi," and "transcends Being and Nonbeing" describes "the Gateway of Birth and Death."

This means that Il-Won-Sang Truth, while being a state of Samādhi, is not just a state of Samādhi, but also a Gateway of Birth and Death that gives and takes as it manifests a myriad of changes. In the Daodejing, this type of Gateway of Birth and Death that transcends Being and Nonbeing is called the "Gateway of the manifold mysteries," meaning a Gateway that gives forth and draws a myriad of wondrous things.

Lao Tzu's Daodejing includes the words, "Heaven and Earth do not act from any wish to be benevolent; they manage all things as 'grass in the field'". Here, "Heaven and Earth" refer to Truth—Il-Won-Sang Truth administers all phenomena from a position of transcendence that does not differentiate things as good or bad, useful, or useless. The words "manages all things as 'grass in the field'" do not mean that all things are treated carelessly, but that all things are treated according to their own circumstances, without any attachment or bias. When a typhoon or avalanche occurs, it is set forth from the Gateway of Birth and Death. If Il-Won-Sang Truth had any attachment to the earth and its features, that would not be possible. It kills what is to be killed and preserves what is to be preserved without bias.

In the Huangdi Yinfujing, we read "Heaven creates, and Heaven kills. This is the principle of The Way." This means that Heaven has a principle, and that it is based on this principle that it kills and creates all things. We could say that this principle is none other than the Gateway of Birth and Death.

There was once a famous Buddhist monk in Jangseong. When his students would ask him for dharma instruction, he would sit on the dharma seat, rap his dharma staff, and remain quiet for a while, before finally stepping down. He would consistently deliver his dharma instructions without speaking, which frustrated his students. One day, they asked him, "Seunim, give us a dharma instruction with words next time."

"Oh! Good idea," he replied cheerfully.

Once again, he gathered the students to give a dharma instruction. This time, after rapping his dharma staff, he sat quietly for a long time before saying, "A caterpillar transforms into a butterfly and flies away." He then stepped down from the dharma seat.

Unable to grasp the meaning of his instruction, the students said, "Seunim, please be more specific."

The monk said, "How can I speak the Truth more specifically than that?"

Have you understood the two dharma instructions, the one without words and the one with words? The monk showed his students the realm of Samādhi that cannot be expressed in words by providing a wordless instruction, and he gave them instruction on the Gateway of Birth and Death by telling them that "a caterpillar transforms into a butterfly and flies away." Yet the students did not grasp the meaning.

When Master Naong went to China, he went to see Master Pingshan Chulin.

"Where do you come from?" Master Chulin asked him.

"I studied under a man named Jigong."

"What does this Jigong do?"

"He wields thousands of swords. He uses a great sword in a harmonious way."

"Let go of Jigong's sword. What does your sword look like?"

At that, Master Naong picked up his cushion and struck Master

Chulin. As Master Chulin fell over, he cried out, "That damnable thief is striking me."

Master Naong then quickly helped Master Chulin to his feet, bowed to him, and said, "I use the Thousand Swords. I can give life as I will, and I can take it away."

Hearing these words, Master Chulin finally gave his authentication. "Your eyes are now open," he said.

In expressing the realm of Samādhi or Nonbeing, the enlightened ones of old often did extraordinary things, such as striking someone with a stick or pushing the person over. But when expressing the realm of Being, or the Gateway of Birth and Death, they observed etiquette with great care.

To the awakened people whose wisdom eyes are open, the meaning of these extraordinary actions is obvious, but to the unawakened people whose wisdom eyes are closed, these actions may seem threatening or theatrical.

If we wish to understand the Gateway of Birth and Death most easily, we should look to the functioning of the mind. When at rest, the mind is in the realm of Samādhi. But when a thought arises, the mind is in the Gateway of Birth and Death.

When the mind is active, the Gateway of Birth and Death is the karmic principle of cause and effect that responds to our virtuous acts or to our transgressions.

We must know how to find Il-Won-Sang Truth inside our mind rather than outside. We may seek outside our mind until our eyes pop out of our heads, to no avail, but if we just look inside our mind we find it easily.

CHAPTER 2

IL-WON-SANG TRUTH IS THE ORIGIN OF ALL THINGS

"It is the origin of Heaven and Earth, parents, fellow beings, and laws, and the original nature of all buddhas, enlightened masters, unenlightened people and sentient beings."

I mentioned before that although Truth is one, Il-Won-Sang Truth has two aspects: essence and function. Essence is the realm that neither arises nor ceases, and function is the karmic principle of cause and effect. The Founding Master called the single Truth possessing these two aspects the "Realm of the Great." This realm is the origin of the Fourfold Grace and the original nature of all living creatures.

The single Truth of Oneness that governs the universe is expressed in two different ways. When referring to all things in the universe we use the word "origin." When referring to living creatures we use the term "original nature." Let us now consider where that single Il-Won-Sang Truth dwells.

Christianity tells us that God exists in Heaven. That is why all churches soar upward toward the sky. Perhaps God was depicted as being in the sky because it was an explanation tailored to the world view of the time.

Where, then, does Il-Won-Sang Truth dwell? The Founding Master said that there is no thing or place among the myriad things in Heaven and Earth and the Dharma Realm of Empty Space where Il-Won-Sang Truth is not to be found. He said that it manifests as the Fourfold Grace of Heaven and Earth, parents, fellow beings and laws. Therefore Il-Won-Sang Truth is the origin of the Fourfold Grace as well as the original nature of all buddhas, enlightened masters, average people, and sentient beings.

Once, I painted a coarse rendering of Bodhidharma and offered it as a gift to a monk. When he said he was paying homage to Śākyamuni Buddha in the mornings and evenings, my response—half serious, half joking—was to ask him, "If all the myriad phenomena in the universe are buddha, why should you worship only Śākyamuni Buddha?" And on the title line above the Bodhidharma painting I wrote, "Of all the myriad phenomena in the universe, there is none that is not buddha. What, then, am I to pay homage to?"

"It is the origin of heaven and earth, parents, fellow beings and laws"

Il-Won-Sang Truth is the origin of all things in Heaven and Earth, which is, in other words, the Fourfold Grace. All things ultimately return to Il-Won-Sang Truth.

If we trace the waters of Han River in Seoul back to their source, we find that they arise at a small spring somewhere north of Hwacheon and flow down from there. Likewise, if we trace back the original nature of all of us living creatures, as well as the origin of all things—which is to say, the origin of the Fourfold Grace—we find that it lies in Il-Won-Sang Truth.

If we take apart all the things in this universe, and we keep breaking them down further and further, we find what is called the "element." And if we break that "element" down still further, we find what is called the "atom." If we break that atom down, we find protons, neutrons, and electrons. These particles represent the world of the infinitesimal. Yet, they too, are said to be formed by just masses of energy.

If we venture in search of the root of all things, we will find energy.

There is a principle that governs this energy—the Il-Won-Sang Truth. The origin of all things is Il-Won-Sang Truth.

Master Chŏngsan said that our universe is made up of three structures: spirit, energy, and substance. He presented them in that order—spirit, energy, substance—but we will look at them in the reverse order.

Substance refers to foundational matter. It refers to what we can touch and grasp with our hands. But, if we ask what it is that moves this substance, we find that it is nothing other than energy. The green leaves turn yellow and red in the autumn because the cold energy of autumn begins to circulate. When we get upset, the energy in our bodies rises and our faces redden. It is the presence of this energy that causes matter to change and move.

How can we describe the spirit? Spirit refers to a wise principle that moves the universal energy. Because of this principle, the season changes to spring and to autumn. In the spring, the warm yang energy goes to work creating all things, and in the autumn the cool yin energy gathers everything back in.

The Founding Master said that this numinous principle is Il-Won-Sang Truth. Śākyamuni Buddha said that it was the Dharmakāya Buddha; Confucius said that it was Tian, or Heaven; and Jesus called it Jehovah. The names are different, but all refer to this omniscient principle and signify that its foundation is singular. Only by knowing where this one Truth lies can we be certain where our true home is.

Among the "Essential Cases for Questioning," in the Won Buddhism Canon there is one that reads, "The myriad dharmas return to one; to what does the one return?" The myriad dharmas return to Il-Won-Sang Truth that rules over all things. But to what does that one thing return?

In Lao Tzu's Daodejing (*Tao Te Ching*), we find the words, "People emulate the Earth, the Earth emulates The Way, but what does The Way emulate? It emulates nature." In other words, that which returns to one thing returns once again to all things. That one thing is contained within all things.

The Dutch philosopher Spinoza said that God exists within all things in the universe—a perspective called "pantheism." He developed this theory while working on grinding eyeglass lenses, his lifetime occupation.

The 4th century BC Chinese philosopher, Zhuangzi, also explained The Way. One day, he was visited by a friend named Dongguozi who asked him, "Where is The Way?"

"The Way is in the millet and the weeds," came the reply.

Hearing this, Dongguozi said, "Are you making fun of me? I want to know the Holy Way."

"The Way is also in the tiles and the bricks," Zhuangzi replied, "what is called The Way is everywhere."

When we attended sporting events as children, there was always a box seat section where the principal and leading members of the community would sit while they offered praise and issued orders. We, in turn, would follow those orders. But if we imagine the Truth that moves all things in the universe to be sitting in a box seat ordering everyone about, we have not yet understood Truth.

As a child, I believed there was something present deep within the ground that sent spring water gushing forth and supplied warmth. A few years ago, I read a newspaper article that described how a spaceship had studied the moon and had found only dust. The article explained that the person managing the study had believed that God was in Heaven, so he was bitterly disappointed to learn there was nothing but dust on the moon. Ultimately, he committed suicide.

The Truth lies in all things. In other words, all the myriad phenomena in the universe are The Way. Since it is the origin of all things, The Way does not exist in any one place, but is present within all things. Il-Won is the Fourfold Grace, and the Fourfold Grace is all the myriad phenomena in the universe.

A student once went to visit Suun, the founder of Cheondoism, while he was in seclusion in his home.

"Where does the Lord of Heaven you speak of exist?" the student asked.

Suun heard the sound of his daughter-in-law weaving hemp on a loom and said, "My daughter-in-law is The Lord of Heaven." That is the origin of the term "innaecheon," or "Humans are Heaven," in Cheondoism. But why would only human beings be "The Lord of Heaven"?

The Founding Master said that all things in this world are buddha, and that when we interact with them we should make buddha offerings to them as if we were honoring the Buddha. Each of us needs to understand and awaken to the fact that the chair we are sitting on now is buddha, Il-Won-Sang Truth, and one and the same as the origin of all things.

"... and the original nature of all buddhas, enlightened masters, unenlightened people, and sentient beings."

Il-Won-Sang Truth is the original nature of all living creatures. The Way is ever-abiding and unextinguished within our minds. The Founding Master told us, "Our original mind is Il-Won-Sang Truth" and that "not only people but all things are buddha and Hanullim, the Lord of Heaven."

Il-Won-Sang Truth dwells within our minds. It was there long ago, it is there now, and it will be with us in the distant future. The easiest way to find Il-Won-Sang Truth, our original mind, is to look within our minds. The Founding Master tells us not to seek the Truth outside, but to seek it within the mind.

When we commit a misdeed, we feel discomfort in our conscience. When we try to tell a lie, our face grows red and our heart races. Why should this be? It is because the Truth Buddha within our minds is carefully guiding us.

This curious buddha called "conscience" is present within every buddha, every average person, every sentient being, every animal of lower development. Buddha nature is not something that is less present in tiny insects and more present in buddhas. It is equally present in all. Viewed from that realm, all beings are equal.

The Chinese character for nature (性), if separated into its component parts, indicates the place where the mind (心) emerges (生).

Where do thoughts arise? Thoughts form in our empty mind. Once formed, they linger for a span of time before ceasing to exist.

Sometimes, a violent mind will subside, and other times a subtle mind will combine with other conditions to transform into a mighty will. Within the flow of time, these thoughts go away, leaving us wondering whether we ever had them at all.

This aspect of mind that arises and then ceases is called the changing mind. There is another aspect of mind, the original mind from which the fluctuating thoughts arise. The Founding Master called this kind of mind that "neither arises nor ceases" the "original mind." This original mind is said to be Il-Won-Sang mind.

The original mind has two aspects, as we read in the Il-Won-Sang Vow: the origin, which is the realm of Samādhi—or true emptiness—and the Gateway of Birth and Death that is subject to sensory conditions—or marvelous existence.

In China, the Zen monk Huineng awakened to The Way and embarked on a life of wandering to avoid the eyes of the envious. One day, he arrived at a temple. As it happened, the monks there had split into two sides and were having a debate.

Seeing a flag waving in the wind, the monks on one side said that the flag was moving, and the monks on the other side said that the wind was moving. The "moving flag monks" were pointing to the effect, and the "moving wind monks" were pointing to the cause.

Huineng said, "It is your minds that are moving."

What meaning could an object have in our lives if we did not perceive it? We perceive objects because of the way the mind functions. Happiness, or misfortune, depends on the functioning of each individual's mind, even regarding the question of whether or not an object exists—the object is perceived differently according to the way each individual mind functions.

The mind is the origin of everything in our lives.

This is what the Buddha meant when he said, "All things are created by the mind." If we awaken to the way our minds function, we awaken to Il-Won-Sang mind within.

Our minds are filled with all manner of notions. When we examine them closely, we see that each of these notions has a birth date—each arose at a specific moment, so each has a specific age. Since all mind notions arise, they also disappear, regardless of their source. We may say that these notions are the "mind that arises and ceases." Yet, the original mind that presides over these arising and ceasing minds is eternal—Il-Won-Sang mind is itself eternal life.

A monk once asked Master Guizong, "Who is the Buddha?"

"You are the buddha," Guizong replied.

The monk's wisdom eyes began to open to these words and he asked, "Then how do I keep my mind free from internal disturbances and external temptations? How am I to preserve my buddha nature?"

Guizong replied, "When there is a single speck of dust in your eye, the illusion flower blooms." In other words, we can only preserve our buddha nature once we are free from our fixation on and attachment to all things.

CHAPTER 3

THE CHANGING AND IMMUTABLE CREATIVE TRANSFORMATIONS OF IL-WON-SANG TRUTH

"Il-Won manifests as both permanence and impermanence. Viewed as permanence, Il-Won unfolds into an infinite world that is spontaneous and ever-abiding just as it is.
Viewed as impermanence, Il-Won unfolds into infinite worlds through the cycle of formation, duration, decay and extinction of the universe, and the birth, aging, illness, and death of all beings. According to how we use our minds and bodies in the four forms of birth as we transform through the six realms of existence, we progress or regress, giving rise to grace from harm, or harm from grace."

The passage in the Il-Won-Sang Vow that begins with "Il-Won manifests as both permanence and impermanence" and ends with "According to how we use our minds and bodies in the four forms of birth as we transform through the six realms of existence, we progress or regress, giving rise to grace from harm, or harm from grace" could be described as an explanation of how Il-Won-Sang Truth manifests creative transformations in all things over time, and how it directs all existence.

As we engage in our practice to become one with Truth, we may understand solely that it is the origin of all things. In the passage above, the Founding Master is teaching us a deeper Truth, namely that Il-Won-Sang Truth endlessly manifests creative transformations, both changeable and immutable, not just at this moment but through the eternity of time and space.

Let us examine each part of this passage and learn its principles.

"Il-Won manifests as both permanence and impermanence"

To begin with, Il-Won-Sang Truth is said to "manifest as both permanence and impermanence." In other words, it is that which never changes when viewed from a perspective of no change, and that which is ever-changing when viewed from a perspective of change.

The word "permanent" refers to the whole of Truth; that immutable realm that Sotaesan called the Realm of the Great. The word "impermanent" refers only to the changeable realm of Truth, called the Realm of the Small.

In short, Il-Won-Sang Truth is one, yet it has two aspects. When viewed from a realm of no change, it is permanence, and viewed from a realm of change, it is impermanence. In other words, it exists forever without change when viewed from the perspective of the realm of Samādhi beyond words and speech, and it is constantly changing, creating, and nurturing all things, when viewed from the perspective of the Gateway of Birth and Death that transcends Being and Nonbeing.

To summarize, Il-Won-Sang Truth is permanent and yet impermanent, impermanent, and yet permanent. This means that it is both the realm of Samādhi and the Gateway of Birth and Death, where the harmonious realm of the Gateway of Birth and Death brings about the changes of creative transformation without departing from the Samādhi state.

"Viewed as permanence…"

Let us first learn about the permanent aspect of Il-Won-Sang Truth. This phrase could be interpreted as giving us a picture of the immutable creative transformations of Il-Won-Sang Truth.

The Founding Master saw Il-Won-Sang Truth as permanent—a realm without change—and said that Il-Won unfolds into an infinite world that is spontaneous and ever-abiding just as it is. This means that when viewed from the perspective of permanence, Il-Won-Sang Truth manifests itself just as it is, unchanging throughout all ages, in both temporal and spatial terms.

For this reason, this realm is also called Il-Won-Sang Truth's Realm of the Great. This means that Il-Won-Sang Truth is ever-present without changing, without arising or ceasing, while it generates creative transformations in all things. Because Il-Won-Sang Truth is not born somewhere, because it did not begin at some point, it is said to be an entity that neither arises nor ceases, that never goes away nor ends.

Imagine a balloon. The balloon is filled with air. But what happens when you press one side of the balloon with your finger? The balloon bulges outward on the other side, right? This may be what scientists call the Law of Conservation of Mass, which implies that, while in a closed system, mass can be rearranged in space, but it can neither be created nor destroyed. This is the way of Il-Won-Sang Truth when viewed in terms of the universe as a whole—the Realm of the Great.

Buddhists have a saying: "It was so in the old days, it is so now, and it will be so in the future. The past, present, and distant future are always in the same place." What this says is that even if Heaven and Earth are turned upside down, so that Heaven becomes Earth and Earth becomes Heaven, Il-Won-Sang Truth remains just as it is, unchanging.

Viewed from another perspective, however, all things do change. Among all things that exist in the universe, there is none that does not change within the flow of time. Yet, throughout this continuous change, the whole remains as it is.

In the Heart Sutra, we find the words, "Neither increasing nor decreasing." Il-Won-Sang Truth always remains just as it is; it does not increase, nor does it decrease. Truth does not appear simply because the world comes into being, and should the world come to an end, Truth will not go anywhere. The Truth itself is eternal and without end, regardless of what happens.

In old China, there was a man named Layman Pang. One day, he set out for a morning walk with his daughter Lingzhao. He saw a drop of dew on a blade of grass and recited the words of a song: "The bright, shining dew upon the grass is the same as the bright, shining meaning of the enlightened master."

Hearing his song, Lingzhao said sarcastically, "This yellow-toothed fellow says all kinds of crazy things."

At his daughter's jibe, Layman Pang asked, "So what would you say?"

And just as he had done, she sang, "The bright, shining dew upon the grass is the same as the bright, shining meaning of the enlightened master."

"The bright, shining dew upon the grass is the same as the bright, shining meaning of the enlightened master." In other words, these two things have the same origin. Il-Won-Sang Truth is not something that is less present in the average person or sentient being and more present in the Buddha. The unchanging Truth is present equally within all things.

Lately, we have seen many astonishing things with the development of genetic engineering. In the past, we thought the gene was something found only in reproductive cells. But it was proven not long ago that with modern advancements in genetic engineering technology, we are now capable of extracting genes from any cell in the body. After seeing this in the news, I thought to myself, "So Il-Won-Sang Truth has been scientifically proven."

WHEN A LEAF FALLS IN THE AUTUMN WIND

A monk once asked his teacher, "What is the most fundamental principle of the buddhadharma?"

The teacher answered, "The body is exposed by the iron wind."

Here, "wind" refers to the autumn wind, termed iron wind because it brings a metallic energy. "The body is exposed by the iron wind" means that the leaves fall away in the autumn wind, and only the foundation remains.

We carry with us all sorts of thoughts as we live our lives. When we cleanse our mind in accordance with the principle of "the body is exposed by the iron wind"—having asked ourselves, "Am I to live my life carrying these random thoughts?"—all that remains is our true nature, revealed just as it is. When we speak of that state before birth or death, where nothing arises nor ceases, we are referring to that realm of the fundamental principle of buddhadharma.

Il-Won-Sang Truth is eternal. It dwells within all things. It exists without beginning or end, the same in the distant past, the present, and the distant future. The Founding Master termed this "eternal existence over an eternity of Heaven and Earth." In other words, Heaven and Earth are eternal.

Why are Heaven and Earth eternal? Truth is eternal. Heaven and Earth, too, are Truth; therefore, they are eternal. The Founding Master said regarding Truth, "It perpetually shines alone as everything passes into extinction over countless ages." We must strive to see that realm of Truth revealed.

Truth has infinite life. When we recite the Buddha's name, we chant the words "Na-Mu Ah-Me-Tah-Bul." "Na-Mu" means "return," while "Ah-Me-Tah-Bul" means "limitless life and limitless light," or the Truth that possesses eternal life.

Because Truth dwells eternally within our own minds as well, the meaning of "Na-Mu Ah-Me-Tah-Bul" is a declaration that we will return to that place of inner Truth. Truth is eternal. I, too, live my life based on that eternal Truth. From this, we can understand two things: Truth is eternal, and our essence is also eternal.

Viewed from its own realm, Truth lies within all things, past, present, and future—it unfolds into an infinite world that is spontaneous, just as it is.

A student once asked a monk, "Who is the Buddha?"

"You are the buddha," the monk answered.

"Then how shall I preserve the buddha?"

To which the monk very simply replied, "Do not entertain harmful states of mind. Then you are preserving the buddha."

What about you? Have you found that just-as-it-is buddha inside that neither arises nor perishes?

We grow accustomed to living within a fixed concept of time in which all things begin, exist, and end, and we accumulate life experiences based on these temporal units. Yet if we look more deeply, we will see that every beginning follows a previous end, and every end presages a new beginning.

In the Huangdi Yinfujing, there is a passage that reads, "Birth is the origin of death, and death is the origin of birth." Spring is at the end of winter and winter is at the end of autumn—each of the four seasons connects with the next, in an endless cycle. We can understand eternity in terms of these changes in phenomena. Il-Won-Sang Truth causes these changes in the realm of existence that is eternally present.

"Viewed as impermanence…"

Up until this point, we have looked at the unchanging realm of Il-Won-Sang Truth—that is, permanence. Now we will learn about impermanence—its changing aspect.

The Il-Won-Sang Vow contains the words "viewed as impermanence, Il-Won unfolds into an infinite realm." In Korean, the word that means impermanence—musang—consists of two parts: mu, meaning without, and sang, meaning always. In other words, there is no constancy—things change.

In the past, Buddhists focused mainly on describing a realm without change—the realm of Nonbeing. But while it is necessary to understand the realm without change for the sake of a future world of greater awareness, we can only go about creating a richer and more vigorous life when we understand the realm of change.

"… Il-Won unfolds into infinite worlds through the cycle of for-

mation, duration, decay and extinction of the universe..."

How does Il-Won-Sang Truth change the universe?

When spring comes, leaves sprout from the ginkgo tree, all frail and tender. At a later time, the tree colors its leaves green, then yellow. At a certain point, they fall away and disappear. But one thing is clear, a leaf is not something that was nonexistent and suddenly came into being. It just sprouted and grew through the absorption of water and nutrients when the conditions were right.

It is the same with all things. The universe initiates formation, lingers on to a time of duration of what was formed, then gradually approaches decay and finally the formation disappears into emptiness.

It is said that our Earth has now passed through its formation eon and is currently in its duration eon. It will linger here for another few billion years. After that, it will gradually begin to decay before finally disappearing. This does not mean that the Earth will simply disappear and that will be that. It will, instead, change into another form.

Cosmologists say that there was a time when all matter existed in the form of a vast, single mass of gas. That would have been the stage of decay of the universe.

All things would have slowly begun to form anew amid a state of total emptiness, during which the Earth would have slowly started to take on its present form. This process of formation, duration, decay and extinction, has its origin in Il-Won-Sang Truth.

Recently, South Koreans have had the opportunity to actually see the beautiful Mt. Kumkang in North Korea. It is a mountain of fantastic shapes of rocks and stones, with all its earth washed away—only rocks are left. People enjoy its beauty. But when I saw Mt. Kumkang, I thought to myself, "It really is old." It is essentially passing through its decay eon right now. I had the sense that Mt. Kumkang, too, would disappear underwater before long—into nothingness.

Mt. Jiri, in contrast, is far younger than Mt. Kumkang. It is earthy and rounded. Within the flow of time, Mt. Jiri, too, will ultimately become an old mountain with nothing but stone left, just like Mt. Kumkang.

In this way, rivers and mountains also pass through the stages of formation, duration, decay, and extinction. I am told that there is a place in Hawaii where a new mountain is being formed amid rumbling earthquakes and erupting volcanoes. This is what we call the formation eon. Il-Won-Sang Truth manifests creative transformations through formation, duration, decay, and extinction. All things and all of nature transform through these four stages within the flow of time.

It takes a very long time for the universe to progress through formation, duration, decay and extinction. One might say that it is no unit of time that we can conceive of, but rather an unlimited unit of time that goes beyond our wildest imagining.

THE PRINCIPLE OF CHANGE IN THE UNIVERSE

This world may be vast, but when we look at it closely we can see that its movements are like the clenching and unclenching of a fist. Winter could be described as the clenching, spring as a slight unclenching. Summer would be when the fingers are splayed out fully, and autumn would be a loosely closed fist. In other words, it changes through the stages of formation, duration, decay, and extinction according to the principle of alternating predominance of yin and yang.

There is something that makes things the way they are, and that something is "causes and conditions." When the river flows, when the clouds scud, when steam rises, when people move, all of these are merely phenomena. The reason that these phenomena happen is none other than Il-Won-Sang Truth.

There is a curious principle in this world—things appear in many varieties with their own distinctive forms, yet none can escape the curious principle of the Gateway of Birth and Death. All changes in this universe pass through formation, duration, decay and extinction, directly influenced by the Three Wheels of Water, Fire, and Wind. It is due to this influence that the Earth has eroded and new mountains have formed.

If we look at China's Yellow River, we see grains of yellow loess mixed into its waters. This loess is said to travel a long distance before settling on Korea's West Sea coast. As a result, the tidal flats on the West Sea are constantly growing, creating large areas of new land.

Wind that has been heated at the earth's equatorial regions turns into a typhoon that moves implacably toward colder regions. As it moves, various things move with it. The rain falls to moisten the Earth, and that rain creates changes on the earth's surface. Oddly enough, water is cold due to yin energy, while fire, being hot, is subject to the influence of yang energy.

As we all know, the oceans undergo rising and falling tides with the motion of the moon, due to the moon's effects on the Earth's water energy. Fire energy, too, is subject to the influences of the sun—most forest fires happen in the summer. Between these two energies of water and fire, the wind arises to influence objects and cause changes in them. Together, all these changes are called the formation, duration, decay and extinction of the universe.

But while the Three Wheels of Water, Fire, and Wind seem to change the universe through those four stages of phenomenological progression, a closer look shows us that these wheels are themselves regulated by two fundamental energies: yin and yang. These two energies are a Truth that corresponds to the two aspects of Il-Won-Sang—the Gateway of Birth and Death that transcends Being and Nonbeing and the karmic principle of cause and effect.

Nothing in the universe escapes the influence of the seasons—spring, summer, autumn, and winter. In spring the yang energy begins to flourish and in summer it is full flight; in autumn the yin energy begins to prevail; and in winter it thrives. Ultimately, the yin and yang energies create the four seasons through their interactions. The Founding Master called this the principle of alternating predominance of yin and yang.

The universe is vast and infinite, yet it cannot escape the Truth of the creative transformations wrought by the principle of alternating predominance of yin and yang. Based on the Truth of this principle, the universe is constantly changing as it unfolds into an infinite world according to the sequence of formation, duration, decay, and extinction.

"... the birth, age, sickness, and death of all beings ..."
What causes an earthquake or any other natural upheaval?
In general, we say that we receive divine retribution when we

commit a transgression. In the case of an earthquake or other natural upheaval, retribution for a transgression is not the factor. Instead, the same principle of Il-Won-Sang Truth manifests itself in the changing aspect of nature—in this case, in an effort of the earth to regain its balance.

Why does a person grow old? Because of the workings of Il-Won-Sang Truth. Birth, age, sickness and death—both in natural phenomena and in humans—are the manifestations of the same principle of Il-Won-Sang Truth.

There was once a famous Confucian scholar in the late Joseon Dynasty. One day, a gentleman told this scholar about a train that traveled between the cities of Hanyang (today's Seoul) and Chemulpo (today's Incheon). The gentlemen said that the train was pitch black, spewed huge clouds of smoke, and was tremendously strong, strong enough to carry many people.

Hearing this, the scholar's students took him to Seoul Station to see the train. The train let out a mighty roar as it pulled into the station. The scholar stared blankly before finally saying, "I thought it would be something special, but now I see that it moves through yin and yang energy."

In other words, the reason the train moved was not because it had some special characteristics, but because of the principle of alternating predominance of yin and yang. The train moved by using the force generated as yin pulls on yang and yang pulls on yin. The same is true for all things—they operate according to the principle of alternating predominance of yin and yang.

When we inhale and exhale, our respiration follows the same principle. When we feel tired at night and we sleep, we do so because the yin energy is flourishing. And when we move about tirelessly during the day, we do so because the yang energy is flourishing.

Our central nervous system has two different systems to spur our responses to stimuli with either sleepiness or wakefulness—the parasympathetic and sympathetic nervous system respectively. The sympathetic nervous system sparks our yang energy, so we feel awake and tense and want to move. The parasympathetic nervous system sparks our yin energy, so we want to sleep and rest. When the sympathetic system has been active, the parasympathetic system appears to say, "It's time to rest now," and sleepiness overcomes us. Because we have yin and yang energies, we experience action and rest as these energies change in response to cause and effect.

For all its size, the earth is subject to centripetal and centrifugal forces. With centripetal force, energy concentrates and pulls toward the earth's axis, while centrifugal force is the energy that seeks to send what is at the center to the outside. The earth harbors these two energies, outward-directed and inward-directed, in an appropriate balance. The constricting energy is the yin energy, and the expanding energy is the yang energy. In short, the earth has an appropriate harmony of yang and yin energy.

During my time as Section Chief of the Department of General Affairs, I once bought a moktak, a wooden clacker. A moktak only produces sound when it has a groove cut into it. With some moktaks, the groove is too narrow, and they do not generate a sound. So, I used a saw to cut a groove into the moktak. Later, I learned that the reason why the moktak would not produce sound was that wood also has a center, so it contracts toward that center. All principles work in the same way.

Let us look at and study the principles behind the phenomena of formation, duration, decay and extinction, or birth, age, sickness, and death. We need to awaken to the fact that Il-Won-Sang Truth is the driving force behind these changes.

There are a truly great variety of animals, plants, and inanimate objects present on this planet, and they are constantly changing—never resting for a moment.

The sequence of change—birth, aging (wear and tear), sickness (breakdown), and death (extinction)—are creative transformations deriving from the karmic principle of cause and effect.

"... According to how we use our minds and bodies in the four forms of birth as we transform through the six realms of existence, we progress or regress."

I will now discuss the changes among the four types of birth. The four types of birth are categorized according to the ways in which living creatures are born: embryo-born, egg-born, moisture-born, and metamorphic.

Humans are born with an umbilical cord, so we call them "embryo-born sentient beings." A chick is born from an egg, so we call it an "egg-born sentient being." A mosquito breeds in damp places, so we call it a "moisture-born sentient being." A caterpillar becomes a chrysalis and the chrysalis becomes a moth, so we call them "metamorphic sentient beings."

These living creatures progress and regress among the six destinies according to how they use their minds and bodies.

The six destinies are stages categorized according to the way beings live their lives. There are three stages where there is only a spirit and no body—heavenly beings, asuras and hungry ghosts. There are another three where a body is also present—human beings, animals, and denizens of hell.

So, what makes them be reborn as humans, or as beasts, or ghosts? Each living creature from one of the four types of birth either progresses among the six destinies toward becoming a heavenly being or regresses toward becoming a denizen of hell, in accordance with the way it uses its mind and body.

The effects of all our deeds accumulate like seeds in both our bodies and minds. In Sanskrit, this is called "karma." The entire reality of our lives—our character, our living conditions—could be described as evidence of this power of karmic action.

We do not become women because we wish to be women or men because we wish to be men—we become women or men according to karmic ties from our previous lives. We are not tall because of a wish to be tall, but because of deeds in a previous life. Likewise, we are not ugly because of a wish to be ugly, but because of deeds in a previous life.

We created karma as a product of the mental and bodily functioning of previous lives, and the result that we see now arose out of that karma.

How much free will do we really have? People often talk of "fortune" or "destiny" in an attempt to explain what happens beyond our will. "Destiny" is the result of our mental and bodily functions during a previous life that are shaping our current destiny. For this reason, the way we use our minds and bodies is of great importance for our eternal life.

The effects of our mental and bodily functioning do not appear right away. They linger as seeds of good or evil in a karma storehouse called ālayavijñāna, very deep within our minds.

These seeds are called "causes," and they will manifest at the right time as "effects."

If we harbor a great deal of hatred or resentment toward others in our minds, many seeds of resentment and hatred for others scatter and become planted in our mind-field. Then, when we receive a body for our next life, we find seeds of resentment and hatred sprouting despite ourselves, and we become the kind of person who always finds fault in others.

When the persimmon leaf falls in the autumn, it awaits to become another persimmon leaf in the coming year. How large or small that new leaf will become is determined by the amount of sunlight and nourishment it will receive in the following year. The bud that absorbs a lot of nutrients will be a large leaf, and the one that absorbs few will end up limp and feeble. This is what we mean when we speak of "cause."

Human beings believe themselves to be in charge when they speak and use their bodies. We have referred to mental and body functioning as the "use of the body and mind." The results of our use of body and mind are stored before they manifest the next time around.

Now, I will explain in more detail the result: karma.

THE WORLD OF THE ĀLAYAVIJÑĀNA

At the very bottom of our minds is the ālayavijñāna, the storehouse of karmic seeds. Everything we do in our present lives, which is the result of the way we use our bodies and minds, is stored there. This dormant karma is a sleeping force. When it finally emerges, it arises with the power to kill a person, or the power to love a person. This is the power of karmic action.

When the karmic power to kill someone is present in our minds, it is a force that compels us to kill that person at all costs, even if we risk our own life. Such is the power of karmic action. We call it karmic force. This karmic force blinds us—we cannot see the Truth in front of our eyes.

How, then, does karmic power form? It forms according to the way we use our body and mind.

When a plane crashes, the first thing investigators do is look for the black box. Similarly, there is a black box storing karmic power within our minds. If we locate it and open it up to see what is inside, we will find a truly vast array of things. We will be able to see whether it contains the predisposition to become a buddha or the predisposition to become a thief.

We can divide this karma into two main types: unshared karma and shared karma. Unshared karma is the karma we create for ourselves, and shared karma is karma we create with others.

Imagine the Jang family. Within this group of people, every Jang individual creates shared karma within the framework of "the Jangs." If some other person starts a quarrel questioning one Jang's rightness about some matter, all the Jangs rise up together. Why do they do this? Because they have created shared karma. All of you sitting here at this moment are hearing the same lecture from me. You are having nearly identical thoughts and using your bodies in nearly identical ways. This is the creation of shared karma.

Many Koreans dislike the Japanese. This is because they have created shared karma. On the one hand, every Korean has his own way of thinking and creates individual or unshared karma based on that way of thinking. Yet, if we were to change bodies and be born again as an American in the next life, we would only be American in body—we would want to come to Korea, to live in Korea, and to take the Korean side on issues.

For such people, it is worth considering their previous lives. If they created shared karma as Koreans in the past and then were reborn in this life as Americans or Japanese, they would long for Korea and side with Korea because they have a history from a past life.

SELF-CAUSED CHAMBER AND OTHER-CAUSED CHAMBER

Even as we create shared karma in this way, the results differ slightly depending on how each of us uses our body and mind. For this reason, unshared karma is bound to appear even among those who possess shared karma. Our children have created shared karma, but they assume slightly different forms depending on their unshared karma. There is a storehouse that collects the creation of shared and unshared karma. Each of these types of karma has its own storage chamber.

First, there is what we will call the "self-caused chamber." I sow seeds in this chamber when I use my mind and body. For instance, each of us has a different character. When I was younger, my classmates nicknamed me "Slowpoke." My mother would always say to me, "Would you speed up a bit before it starts to rain?"

"You were just born to move slow," she would sigh.

Perhaps the reason I move so slowly is that I engaged in many slow actions in a previous life, so I planted a lot of slowpoke seeds in my self-caused chamber. With all the easygoing seeds that I have already planted in this lifetime, I am certain to be even more of a slowpoke in the next. So, I am now working to break that habit during this lifetime.

Each of us has a different character and different gifts. Some of us have great skills, some are stylish, some have fire in their eyes, some have keen noses, and some have bright eyes. My younger brother was born to the same parents as me, but every aptitude test that he takes shows him to be oriented toward science and engineering.

I can see that my brother is very quick with calculations. As for me, I studied the humanities and am slow with numbers. Some people are good at baduk, and some are good at brush calligraphy. One set of parents will have children with completely different gifts.

If I deliver a lot of lectures in this life, people will call me a gifted speaker in the next. But if someone commits a lot of thefts in this life, that person will have a tendency toward thievery in the next as well. When we use our minds and bodies here and now, we must make a clear determination to know whether we are planting slowpoke seeds or neurotic seeds in our self-caused chamber, planting the seeds of buddhahood and the gift for harmony, or planting the seeds for alienating others.

A person who is impatient by nature acts with impatience. Spendthrift persons feel compelled to spend money even when they have none. In this way, each person's overall character is created according to the self-caused chamber. This is why it is important to understand that our face, our personality, our talents are the result of the emergence in this life of seeds planted in the ālayavijñāna in our previous lives.

Second, there is the other-caused chamber. These are the seeds sown by others. For example, if I am good to this person seated in front, a seed is planted in his other-caused chamber—the thought of "Rev. Jang EungChul was really kind to me." If we meet again in the next life, the seed of my having been good to him in this life will come to the surface and sprout.

Conversely, if I do terrible things to him, a different seed is planted in his other-caused room—the thought of "Rev. Jang EungChul is a truly nasty person." When I try to do something with him in the next life, that seed will sprout up, and he will pay me back by doing harm to me—perhaps, he will look at me askance and say to others "Don't trust that guy."

My own other-caused chamber could be described as the place where I store the things planted in my inner mind regarding interactions with other living creatures. If I have done a good job of lecturing, you are storing up happiness related to me in your other-caused chambers, while I am storing blessings to receive from you in my next life. I hope that as you listen to my lecture, I am planting seeds in your other-caused chambers that say, "I'm really grateful to him, I really appreciate this lecture."

If you meet me in your next life, I hope you will find yourself feeling me oddly appealing, wishing to buy me a cup of tea, wishing to help me.

When the seeds planted in the other-caused chambers reveal themselves, some of us reap the rewards of happiness and a positive environment in the next life, while there may be others who are born into an unfortunate environment and are tormented by misfortune.

The seeds planted in the self-caused chamber shape a person's character—his personality, his gifts, and so forth. We develop habits that shape our character. When we create for ourselves seeds that are stored within another person, we reap as we sow—receiving back in kind the good or evil we do to others. This is how we form karmic affinities in our environments.

THE EFFECTS OF KARMA

We create self-karma and other-karma when we use our minds and bodies. Depending on the karma we have created, we progress or regress among the six destinies when we enter a new life. That is why our mental and bodily functioning is of such importance.

We create different types of karma, both consciously and unconsciously.

There is one type of karma that pulls us in one direction or another, depending on the intentions we have established. We are pulled into actions and consequently into their effects, which can be positive or negative. We may, for example, be driven into a human life, male or female, or we may be born as one kind of animal or another. Once we are born, the effects of a different type of karma provide us with the particulars of our new self, such as a pretty or an ugly face, with large or small eyes.

What pulls us in a specific direction is a particular force within our minds—it may be greed, or it may be aspiration.

That force that pulls us is our karma. What are the decisive factors for where and how a person is reborn after he dies? We receive a body according to the attachments we carry. Those attachments are the force that pulls us in a specific direction. So, we may be born into the Lee family or the Park family, we may receive a human body, or we may be born into one of the other five modes of existence, such as the realm of animals or the realm of the hungry ghosts.

When we look closely into our minds, we find a variety of different aspects. The strongest of them is like the commander of our mind—the mind that is making you listen to this lecture today.

Let us then endeavor to understand the consciousness that pulls each of us around every day. If I set a worthy intention for myself, I will use my mind and body in worthy ways. Conversely, if I set an unworthy intention for myself, I will ultimately develop an inferior character and find myself in unsatisfactory circumstances.

Yet, an intention alone is not enough. We also need to reform our habits.

We see families where most of the members have a gentle character, yet there is a child among them who has a rude personality. In such cases there might be a person who habitually engaged in rude behavior in previous lives, but at some point, came to desire gentleness and kindness and wished to incorporate those qualities into his behavior. That yearning became a seed in his mind, to be reborn into a kind and gentle family, which manifested in this present life. If we did not re-form our habits during previous lives, we will be born into a place with a character that sharply differs from our own, and gradually the old behaviors will begin to manifest themselves and create conflict. This is an example of the workings of personal karma.

"... we progress or regress..."

How does the path of progression develop in our present life? As we move along our lives we pass through different levels, or stages: the Elementary Stage, the Stage of Special Faith, the Stage of the Battle Between Dharma and Māra, the Status of Dharma Strong and Māra Defeated, the Status of Beyond the Household, and the Status of the Greatly Enlightened Tathāgata. The latter stage, Greatly Enlightened Tathāgata, occurs once we have attended properly to our mental and bodily functioning. We progress or regress after death depending on the workings of the cycle of the six destinies.

The greatest fortune on our path of progression is to receive a human body. It may seem appealing to be born a heavenly being, but when this happens it is no longer easy for us to create blessings with our virtuous action on the path to buddhahood.

When we are unable to create blessings, we become susceptible to regression. Just as we have to pay more money for a hotel room with better facilities, we need to have accrued many blessings to enter Heaven. A day in Heaven is like several centuries here—Heaven, then, is a place for spending blessings, not creating them.

Revered teachers such as the Founding Master, Master Chŏngsan and Master Daesan emerged in Korea as though stepping through a threshold to open the door for a new age and a new religion. To create a better world, they made promises to one another and formed karmic affinities.

The karmic affinities we create along the Won Buddhism path are not personal relationships—they are relationships with the Founding Master. The buddhas too undertook great efforts to create the order of Won Buddhism. Now that we have found Won Buddhism, we must work hard at mind practice—the proper use of body and mind—so that we can create the right affinities and progress.

Whether we progress or regress depends upon the functioning of our body and mind. Among the people we encounter, we find those who are in a progression period and those who are in a regression period. When we visit other people's homes, we find houses where the energy seems light, and others where the energy seems dense. That means that some houses are in a progression period, and others are in a regression period.

A person in a progression period has a strong determination, is humble, and is deeply committed to contributing to the public good as well as performing acts of generosity. If such a person dies while having been fated to go to a lesser realm, the heavenly beings and asuras will intervene to guide the spirit toward a better place. "Is it right for a person like you who has done such good deeds to go to such a place?" they will ask.

Each of us needs to clearly determine whether we are in fact in a progression period or in a regression period, and to make a vow to set our course toward a progression period.

If we keep finding ourselves making excuses for not doing worthy things, we need to awaken to the fact that we are losing the direction of progression. At that point it is important to gather ourselves and to pray with dedication for guidance to change the functioning of our body and mind.

I once knew a young man who was truly unlovable. Because this person kept acting in an unlovable manner toward others, he was constantly excluded by them. A teacher saw this dynamic and said to him, "I am going to write a prayer for other people. I want you to make offerings with this prayer and practice doing only kind things for others, even if they are small things." The person accepted the teacher's counsel and prayed for three months, and always made sure to be kind to other people. Soon, people began looking at him differently, saying, "This is a truly lovable person."

Even someone who seems to have no lovable qualities can develop them through prayer and move into a progression period, while using body and mind for the benefit of others. Each of us needs to wipe the past clean and think deeply about whether we are benefitting others or harming them.

If someone says to us that we have no generous spirit, we should contemplate this to see if we might be in a regression period. We should then pray for all living creatures and work hard to help other people, even in the smallest ways. If we allow bad habits to influence the way we use our mind, we should say, "I must be in a regression period." And then we need to change the way we have been using our minds, develop good habits, and boldly set our course toward a progression period.

I once heard the following story: a long time ago in ancient China, Emperor Longxi wrote a famous dictionary, which he called the

"Longxi Dictionary of Chinese." Emperor Longxi had no eyebrows, like a leper, and as it turned out, he had been a leper who lived near Luoyang in a past life.

While living as a leper, the emperor always had difficulty finding food, so he began to think, "I should just die." But then he met a monk who said to him, "Instead of wishing to die, why don't you perform charitable acts for others and say prayers for the country's prosperity and the welfare of its people?"

Every time they met, the monk said the same thing. Finally, the leper thought, "Praying is better than dying, even if I have to beg for food." And he prayed and prayed for the country and its people, all the way from the age of sixteen to the age of eighty. Every time he begged for food, he prayed for the person from whom he begged. Although he was a leper, he prayed and lived the life of practice for so long that he earned the name of Laishen—"the leper god." It is said that after he died, he was reborn into a royal family, where he would become Emperor Longxi.

Due to our karmic retribution, we may now be living a humble life, but we can free ourselves from the cycle of the six destinies through the way we use our body and mind. The outcome will depend on whether we use our body and mind for ourselves, or for others and for the country.

When we use body and mind for others, or for the country, the resulting energy is transmitted through a wireless telephone service: Truth.

THE PRINCIPLE OF THE WORLD'S CREATION AND DESTRUCTION, PROSPERITY, AND DECAY

Previously, I explained unshared karma, which we create ourselves, and shared karma, which people create together.

Shared karma describes the karma hidden within each member of a family that lives together and uses body and mind as one in response to sensory conditions.

When observing different family units, we may find distinctive shared consciousness within them. Each family may also have its own value system, which is the manifestation, here and now, of the ways in which the family members used their bodies and minds as one unit while living together in a past life.

Some families are in a process of collapse. We find households that are disintegrating, and others that are prospering with blessings and good fortune. In these cases as well, we must turn our attention to karma from a previous life.

There are instances where, although the head of the family works hard for the sake of all family members, things do not go according to plan. This occurs when, in a previous life, the family members created a negative shared karma, and that effect now comes to fruition.

Yet, if the head of the family is endowed with outstanding capabilities and dharma power, he can have that great misfortune reduced to a significantly smaller one. Likewise, if all of you sitting here today pray and pray for your families, work diligently, and demonstrate leadership ability—say for example, by nurturing the minds of your family members—you and your families can advance in leaps and bounds despite any karmic power from a previous life.

The reliability and leadership capacity of the family's head is a crucial factor here.

This applies also to organizations. The process of creation and destruction, prosperity and decay of an organization is also determined by the result of shared karma—with the spirit of the organization's leader being the most important factor.

The same is true for a country. Korea has not perpetrated atrocities such as invading other countries, but it certainly has experienced much depredation at the hands of its neighbors. We have been forced to endure this misfortune throughout our history. It is likely the case that the effects of jointly created karmic power ultimately account for about 70 to 80 percent of this situation.

Be the past as it may, we continue creating shared karma even now. We Koreans are building the unique cultural consciousness of the "white-clad folk"—as we used to be called in the past. The behavior of the international community affects our sense of well-being, to which we react together with mind and body, despising or welcoming it. Sometimes the results of our reactions may appear immediately and at other times they may remain hidden to linger as shared karma—the corresponding outcome will arrive at some point in the distant future.

Some scholars say that every group of people forms its own cultural consciousness. This is true. Yet, while the shared karmic power of a people is indeed strong, the influence of the individuals who are their leaders, which is dependent on their strength and capabilities, is even greater.

Recently, mass communication has become an element with its

own cultural group consciousness. The leaders in charge of this cultural phenomenon have an increasingly large impact on society and are responsible for much of its shared karma.

Even more so the leaders at the helm of society must be attentive to shared karmic power. If a leader dwells too much on immediate results and creates the wrong sort of karma today, a catastrophe could result in the distant future. A great leader can only create a progressively healthy organization or country when he governs it with a leadership grounded in morality and a sage-like use of the mind.

"... giving rise to grace from harm, or harm from grace..."
The words "giving rise to grace from harm" mean that it is possible for grace to emerge even amid harmful conditions if we use body and mind well. Imagine someone who was born into a very poor and deprived environment. This person makes up his mind and says, "I need to sleep less than other people and work harder because I'm poor." He then goes on to succeed based on hard work. This is an example of creating grace out of harm.

We may be considered visually unattractive, but if we resolve to make up for it through kindness, we can create greater grace for ourselves. But if we use perceived unattractiveness as an excuse to live an unworthy life, we will go from suffering to worse suffering. All of this depends upon how awakened we are in our use of body and mind.

To be precise, what we call "harm" is unwholesome karma that we created in a past life—through improper use of body and mind—that manifests itself as reality when the right conditions arise.

For example, it is always a problem to have an undesirable personality. It is a problem to have a humble appearance. It is a problem to be born into the midst of conflicted human relationships. A poor environment is harmful and painful for most. Yet, it may be the case for some that only part of it is harmful even if everything is painful.

I may live amid a painful environment. Yet, if I awaken to and accept the fact that the harmful environment is the result of what I have made for myself in the past, and if through that acceptance I set the proper direction for my future and commit to a sincere and firm determination, I can use that harm as a sort of fertilizer to transform my situation into a beneficial one.

"I never would have recognized you" we find ourselves saying when we have known someone to be a bit of a rascal, only to meet him again a few years later and find that his mind has developed, so we can now hold him in much higher esteem.

Three things are important here, I believe: a firm will, determination, and the commitment to carry on until our wish is fully realized.

Looking back over the history of Korea, we can see that it has been a history of tremendous hardship. This is evidenced in the following: a small patch of land, a divided homeland, a lack of resources, and—in the aftermath of the Korean War—an unfavorable international environment. Despite this, the ruling and working classes banded together to overcome those difficulties. As a result of this effort, we are now poised to enter the stage of the advanced nations.

This example of Korean history shows that it is possible for grace to be created in a harmful situation.

Conversely, "giving rise to harm from grace" means that it is possible for damaging things to arise out of grace. In other words, if we are neglectful while existing in a place of grace, we may find ourselves facing far more difficult situations ahead.

There are people who have everything—a good home environment, good looks, economic means. But, if they fail to understand the value of these things and develop, instead, the habits of laziness or debauchery, they may be creating their own destruction and that of their families.

When we experience favorable conditions, it means the beneficial karma we stored up from a previous life has come back to us in the form of a positive environment here and now.

But if we have not awakened to the understanding of cause and effect, all the good habits we strived to form in our past life gradually turn into harmful ones—habits such as laziness and wastefulness.

Often, when average people and sentient beings experience a small measure of success, they forget all about their previous difficulties. They bask in their success, only to succumb once again to torment. As the torment deepens, they repeat the process, make new determinations and strive for better results. Yet, it becomes like riding a seesaw—they live their lives moving up and down on the plank of creation and destruction, prosperity and decay.

The person who has awakened to the Truth of eternal life and the Truth of cause and effect knows how to progress toward self-development. Using mind and body to give rise to grace, there's no need to rise and fall on the plank of good and ill fortune. We study and practice Il-Won-Sang Truth in the hope of using body and mind properly so that we may forever progress and enjoy grace in everything.

"... Il-Won unfolds into an infinite realm..."

This phrase tells us that when Il-Won is viewed as permanence it is eternal. We can see it from the perspective of the unchanging infinite realm or from the perspective of the Truth that rules over this changing world. When seen from the perspective of change, this universe remains eternal.

"Viewed as impermanence, Il-Won unfolds into infinite worlds through the cycle of formation, duration, decay and extinction of the universe, and the birth, aging, illness, and death of all beings..."

This phrase is the opposite of the view that sees the world as having a beginning and an end—a beginning when God created it and an end at some future time.

In Won Buddhism doctrine, this changing realm unfolds into infinite worlds that constantly transform in an endless cycle of beginning and end. Continuous interactions between Heaven and Earth transform the universe through a process of formation, duration, decay, and extinction. We also see this in the changes of spring, summer, autumn, and winter, with every beginning transforming into every end in an endless cycle.

It is important to clarify that I am not talking about the turning of a hamster wheel. It is, instead, an eternal continuation, like when winter ends and spring arrives. But while this year's spring is the same as last year's in terms of its being spring, it differs slightly in its content.

The same is true of the stages of formation, duration, decay, and extinction. All things change through a process of birth, aging, sickness, and death within the greater framework of Heaven and Earth.

When I was a child, my family ran a mill. There, you could see one large wheel turning vigorously, and a great number of smaller wheels turning along with it. In the same way, all things are constantly changing based on the larger framework of Heaven and Earth.

Next, there is the world of us, human beings. While our original nature is eternal, existing infinitely without beginning or end, our context and positioning in this reality are forever changing. Yet, these changes center on mental and bodily functions in accordance with the laws of the universe—they proceed eternally, sometimes as progression and sometimes as regression.

What we must note here is that even though the universe and all things change mechanically according to a certain timetable, we human beings may live longer or shorter lives depending on how we use our minds. This is why mind practice is such an important factor in our lives.

When we make proper use of mind and body, we can create positive karma and live for many years, develop an outstanding character, and earn respect. But if we do not manage our mind properly, we will create negative karma and regress.

Are we using our minds for our own selves? Are we using them for our family, our temple, our world? We write our own stories. At this moment, each of us is writing our own history.

The past is gone, and the future has yet to arrive. There is only ever this moment. There is no past, no future. Only this moment. We create our history by the way we use our minds at this very moment.

Have we chosen a direction for our lives? Is it toward desire or toward the pursuit of Truth? We need to set the proper course here and now. We must think and act with a sound mind. Using our mind to benefit others is the path to benefiting ourselves also. Only when we use mind and body to change our bad habits into good ones can we change our course toward progression.

It is invigorating to recall the dharma instruction of Master Chŏng-san: "Engage in proper mind practice and you will become a master in the new world."

Part II

THE PRACTICE OF
IL-WON-SANG

"Therefore, by modeling ourselves on Il-Won-Sang, the Dhar-makāya Buddha, we unawakened beings vow to practice whole-heartedly to cultivate our minds and bodies perfectly; to know human affairs and universal principles perfectly and to use our minds and bodies perfectly, so we can progress rather than regress and receive grace rather than harm, until we attain the awesome power of Il-Won and become one with the nature of Il-Won."

The Founding Master experienced the great enlightenment of Truth and gave it the name of Il-Won-Sang. In the section on Truth, he explained the two realms of Il-Won-Sang Truth—the realm of Samādhi and the Gateway of Birth and Death. He said that Il-Won-Sang is the origin of all things in the universe and the original nature of all living creatures; and that it manifests both as an immutable creative transformation and as changing creative transformations over time in all things in the universe.

It could be said that, in this section on the practice of Il-Won-Sang, the Founding Master explains to later generations how they should become one with Il-Won-Sang Truth in their lives.

The gist of this section is a dharma instruction urging us to embrace

Il-Won-Sang as our object of faith and adopt it as the model for our practice. Il-Won will then guard our minds and guide us in the understanding of human affairs and universal principles. It will instruct us in ways to use our minds properly so that we develop a consummate character. We will gain the awesome power of Il-Won and commit ourselves to becoming one with its substance and nature.

In the past, due to a lack of knowledge, mainstream religious activity consisted of teaching people to believe in one version of the universe according to the scriptures of sages, without any practical inner experience. This could be characterized as "faith religion." But because the world of the future will be one of clear awareness at the individual level, there will be a major emergence of "practice religion"—religion that goes beyond mere faith and extends to belief in and awakening to the Truth of the universe, as well as to the practice of those awakenings in daily life.

As such, the section on practice could also be described as offering an explicit methodology for attaining buddhahood—a life of using the Truth inherent in the universe as our own.

CHAPTER 4

A Life Modeled Wholeheartedly on Il-Won-Sang Truth

"... by modeling ourselves on Il-Won-Sang, the Dharmakāya Buddha, we unawakened beings..."

For those of us unawakened beings who have not yet experienced a direct realization of the Truth, it is most important to adopt the Dharmakāya Buddha, Il-Won-Sang Truth as our object of faith and model for practice, as explained by the Founding Master. We must model our lives after the buddhas and sages.

Let us consider where we place our trust as we live our lives. When troubles arise, we often find ourselves crying out to our parents. This is because we depended upon them from the earliest stages of childhood, and they assumed the place, in our unconscious, of a refuge to turn to in times of trouble.

But even though we may still rely on this trust in our parents, at some point we will need to leave their nest. In my own experience, the despair I felt when I sensed my mother's helplessness was truly devastating.

Usually, when our faith in our parents recedes, it gradually shifts over to our spouse.

Some time ago, the wife of a Won Buddhist acquaintance of mine passed into Nirvana. He told me that he could not bear to enter the room where she had lain on her sickbed. He was unable to do so, he said, because of a feeling of emptiness—it was as though a wall against which he had been leaning had collapsed. The refuge that a wife or husband represents is destined to collapse in the end.

Some people place their focus on their children. But are our children the correct recipients for our hopes and needs? In the end, they too will marry and depart, leaving us with only the sorrow of their parting. Still less can we put our trust in money or possessions, or in glory and power. All of it will at some point collapse, vanish, scatter to the wind.

When we come to depend upon something that we cannot possibly expect to stay with us forever, we are no different than a small child playing house inside a collapsing structure.

To live our lives believing in and depending on what we can touch and see is to plant the seed of misfortune. I recall the lyrics of a popular song from many years ago: "Love is the seed of tears." When we become attached to money, glory and the opposite sex, we may feel pleasure in them, but before long we will be forced to endure the pain of separation from them. Let us avoid such unwise behavior.

Even greater misfortune befalls those who place their faith in superstition. In terms of human history, we have barely lived through our infancy and adolescence. This has made it difficult for high-order religions to accurately teach the faith of Truth to people who have not yet gone farther than the worship of individual sages.

What are we to believe in? In his chapter on "The Founding Motive of the Teaching," the Founding Master instructed us to believe in a religion based on Truth. It may be rational to believe in the teachings of a sage who has achieved awakening, but it is a contradiction to take that sage as an object of faith and pray to him for blessings and happiness.

A sage's power to grant blessings and happiness is limited. We only become sound practitioners if, when performing acts of faith in line with the principles, our object of faith is the realm of Il-Won-Sang Truth, which rules over and transforms all things in the universe.

The Founding Master taught us that even if there are monuments made in someone's image, they should not be turned into objects of worship. Il-Won-Sang is purposely just an image that represents Il-Won as the governing source of all things in the universe. Rather than representing a sage or deity, the circle image points directly to Il-Won-Sang Truth. Won Buddhism enshrines Il-Won Sang in all its temples.

This may be the most revolutionary act in the history of human religion. Now, let us explore the fact that Il-Won faith is somewhat difficult to approach. All of you here surely experienced this in the beginning.

We are predisposed to dedicate our faith to the Buddha image that we can see with our eyes. It is not as easy to dedicate our faith to Il-Won, also called the Dharmakāya Buddha, Fourfold Grace, at first because we cannot see it with our eyes or hear it with our ears. Once we enshrine Il-Won-Sang as our image, we may begin by reciting the words "Dharmakāya Buddha, Fourfold Grace" repeatedly. Over time, when we experience difficult things, trying things, pleasant things or difficulty making decisions, we may begin to pray, and pray again, while contemplating the divinity and mercy of the Dharmakāya Buddha, Fourfold Grace. If we do so, we will eventually come to perceive Il-Won-Sang Truth within our mind. That is the process of coming to serve Il-Won-Sang Truth. When we reach that point, we will feel how the Truth Buddha is always present, protecting us or correcting us when we set upon the wrong path.

When we are committed to a life of faith and we devote ourselves to prayer, we develop a sense of connection with the formless Dharmakāya Buddha, Fourfold Grace.

Truly amazing advances have been realized recently in wireless telephone technology. If it were possible for us to have a cell phone conversation with the Dharmakāya Buddha, as though we were speaking to one another, we might say that we had gained the awesome power of the Truth Buddha.

When a prayer comes from someone who senses the power of the Dharmakāya Buddha, Fourfold Grace, it is answered promptly, so that person's desires come to pass.

BELIEF IN THE TRUTH, DOCTRINE, ORDER, AND TEACHER

If we are to arrive at faith in Truth and we perceive its awesome power, our beliefs will work in unison. These are the Four Great Beliefs of Nonduality: belief in Truth, in the teacher, the doctrine, and the order.

When we practice our faith fervently with these four beliefs, our path to the ultimate stage of faith in Il-Won-Sang Truth will be swift.

When you go to the airport, you can see that an airplane does not immediately soar up into the sky. Instead, it races along the runway before finally making its leap up into the sky. Similarly, there is a preliminary stage of belief if we are to arrive at perfect faith. I am introducing this concept to beginning practitioners so they may trust the foundation of their faith and strengthen it by practicing with other practitioners.

First, there is the belief in our teachers.

Il-Won-Sang Truth is a mysterious absolute—it is never visible to the eye, it makes no sound, gives off no smell, and can never be touched. It is important for us to have a mind of faith oriented toward believing in the dharma power of our teachers and to obey their teachings. The Head Dharma Masters guide us with their belief. They have awakened to and practiced the dharma of the Founding Master, who experienced the great enlightenment of Il-Won-Sang Truth. Their teachings empower us to practice as they have.

Second, there is the profound faith in the order that was created by those awakened teachers.

Without the order, it would be impossible to offer effective succor to the world, and many of us would never receive eternal deliverance. The order is a beacon for humanity and a training ground for attaining buddhahood—it shows the path for sentient beings to become buddha-bodhisattvas. Let us participate in the order with a faith that is united and devoid of discrimination, so we can form a closer affinity with the Buddha. Let us also strive to help the order become a field of blessings, united in reverence of the Buddha's works.

Third, we profess profound and sincere faith in the doctrine, system, and the teachings left for us by the Founding Master.

Let us each strive to become one with the doctrine and develop an appreciation that truly rejoices in and exults the doctrine.

I recall the story of one follower of Won Buddhism. Before this person encountered the faith, a lucky day meant being able to get a free cup of tea from somebody. But after encountering Won Buddhism and commencing study of the Truth of the karmic principle of cause and effect, this person came to believe that the luckiest day was when he was able to perform charitable service for others.

In this way, our values gradually change to conform to the doctrine of Won Buddhism. As our philosophy of life aligns with the teaching of Won Buddhism we evolve into buddha-bodhisattvas and enjoy the respect of others.

Fourth, we must have a belief that is one with Truth.

With each passing day and each passing month, we develop a mind of faith that reveres, relies upon and ultimately becomes one with the Dharmakāya Buddha, Fourfold Grace—the ultimate state of being that exists in nature as well as in our original nature, which shelters, nurtures us, and realigns us when we err or stray from the path.

I mentioned above the mind of faith in Truth.

When we live without belief in the doctrine, teachers, order, and Truth, it is as though we are sailing without knowing to which port we are traveling. It is as though we are walking in the darkness of night without a lamp. But when we proceed with faith, we begin to follow a beacon and we recognize the signposts that appear along the way in the journey of our lives.

There is not a parent in this world who would abandon the children that depend upon and believe in them. When a sentient being has sincere faith in a teacher, that teacher will never desert the student. The sentient being who has faith in the order will never be abandoned by it. And the buddha-bodhisattva who gave us the doctrine will deliver, without exception, to those believers who have sincere faith in it.

When we have limitless faith in the Dharmakāya Buddha, Fourfold Grace, we enjoy the hidden help and virtue of Truth. Let us impress this fact deeply upon our minds. Faith should not be tallied in terms of immediate benefits and gains. Limitless blessings and virtue only come when we have dedicated ourselves to a belief that transcends issues of benefits and gains.

THE AWAKENING OF SENTIENT BEINGS

We must begin by recognizing that we are unawakened sentient beings.

Being unawakened means, first, not knowing that one is buddha; second, not understanding the principle of the cycle of the six destinies and the principle of eternal life; third, being unaware of the existence of the karmic principle of cause and effect; and fourth, not knowing how to escape from this unawakened state. The unawakened state is a lack of knowledge of the dharma of practice and the dharma of creating blessings. It is only when we recognize ourselves to be in this unawakened state that true faith emerges, and we can practice with humble minds.

The *Diamond Sutra* tells us that the person who has observed the precepts and cultivated merits, and has practiced with one buddha, two buddhas, countless buddhas, will love and praise the buddhadharma eternally.

Before the emergence of Won Buddhism there were many sages who emerged in Korea to fulfill the role of preparing the groundwork.

The first of these was Ch'oe Suun, who came to the world in Yongdam, Gyeongju. Suun has been called the "Yongdam god of gratitude," and his role was to show a new possibility for religion, one that aspired to achieve new changes in a traditional Korean society where the customs of the past lay fallow like an abandoned field.

Next, there was Kang Chŭngsan, called the "Donggok god of exorcising resentment." Kang's role was as a major sage in the Donggok area of Jeonju. His activity consisted mainly of resolving grievances and the injustices that had been perpetrated over the years.

Following Suun and Chŭngsan, came the Founding Master, who was called the "Yeongsan and Iksan god of the myriad sages," a presiding sage who would make sages of unawakened beings.

When Śākyamuni Buddha arrived in this world, there had already been many others, including Master Jin'gwi, who had come before to lay the foundation. In Christianity, John the Baptist came into the world and did his work ahead of Jesus Christ.

As these examples show, before the arrival of a great order there are those who come to lay the groundwork. The presiding buddhas arrive later to carry out their work. The work the Founding Master came to do was to initiate a new order and to make sages of sentient beings.

The doctrine of Won Buddhism consists of a method of practice for making all of us into sages. It is important that we understand this fundamental meaning and embark upon our practice by making a vow to escape the unawakened state of sentient beings and become sages.

There was a time when I served directly under Master Daesan. He slept in the main room, and I slept in an attached room to the side. How would I, an unawakened sentient being, have felt serving and sleeping next to Jesus Christ? I will never forget the moment when I considered what an honor it would have been to serve and sleep next to Śākyamuni Buddha. I felt overcome with emotion. "Oh!" I thought. "To be able to serve and sleep next to Master Daesan ..."

In the past, it was difficult to meet sages. The future, however, will be a world in which we shake hands with sages, eat with them and interact with them directly. For this to happen, we need only to open our eyes. It's of no concern where we come from or what our shortcomings are; all that matters is that we firmly resolve to achieve buddhahood through mind practice based on this method.

THE RELATIONSHIP BETWEEN THE DHARMAKĀYA BUDDHA AND IL-WON-SANG

Why did the Founding Master talk about "modeling ourselves on Il-Won-Sang, the Dharmakāya Buddha"? Isn't it a bit odd that he would suddenly start talking about the "Dharmakāya Buddha"?

All the sages of the three periods of past, present, and future have roots. A sage without roots is a second-rate sage. For instance, Jesus traced his roots back to the figure of Moses in Judaism.

But didn't Judaism persecute Christianity terribly? Even so, there were very discerning people among the disciples of Jesus Christ, and Christianity avoided abandoning its roots in Judaism by adopting its scriptures as the Old Testament.

What were the Buddha's roots? Who did he take as his guide? His teacher was Dīpaṃkara Buddha. He is a figure we know of today from Hinduism. Buddhism absorbed a great deal from the Hindu scriptures. Confucius also made it clear that his roots lay in the ideas of Yao, Shun, Yu, Tang, King Wen, King Wu, and the Duke of Zhou.

In other words, a sage without roots can never be a first-rate sage, and his religion will merely be transitory. We can distinguish between temporary religions and eternal ones based on whether they have roots or not. A temporary religion is like a blade of grass that shoots up quickly in the summer but withers away in the fall.

The Founding Master predicted that the world of the future would have a dominant religion whose principal doctrine would be the buddhadharma. However, he also said that it would not be the old Buddhism that had fragmented into different sects, but a new Buddhism adapted to everyday life, the public, and the times.

The great scholars are not those who claim originality, but those who show humility and serve their predecessors, those who studied the teachings of a previous sage and then realized new achievements based on those teachings.

A noted calligrapher will always tell you about the teacher under whom the skill was learned. Religion is no exception to this rule. Even when that sage achieves an original enlightenment, respect must be shown, for those who came before and those who carry on the line that runs through past, present, and future.

The Founding Master was able to claim originality—he presented a system centered on the doctrine of the Fourfold Grace, the Four Essentials, the Threefold Practice, and the Eight Articles, with Il-Won-Sang as the fundamental tenet. The fact that he traced his roots to a predecessor in the form of Śākyamuni Buddha reflects the spirit of great cause that pervades all sages of the triple world of past, present, and future equally—they show their loyalty to their lineage.

There are two sayings frequently used among Buddhists: "The Buddha shines brighter each day," and "The dharma wheel turns again."

"The brilliance of the Buddha increases each day" is used by students of Śākyamuni Buddha. It means that great teachers like Bodhidharma, Huineng, and Venerable Wonhyo carried on the buddha light of Śākyamuni Buddha and worked ceaselessly to make it shine ever brighter.

"The dharma wheel turns again" means to shed new light upon and keep turning the dharma wheel as Śākyamuni Buddha did for Dīpankara Buddha before him.

Before Jesus Christ, there was Moses. We might say that Jesus traced his roots to a previous sage in the form of Moses.

"The brilliance of the Buddha increases each day" indicates transmission in smaller units, and "The Dharma Wheel Turning Again" indicates a give-and-take between presiding sages within a grander scheme, one in which one great era changes completely.

When the Founding Master traced his roots back to Śākyamuni Buddha, it was an example of "The Brilliance of the Buddha Increases Each Day" rather than "The Dharma Wheel Turns Again." We must understand that he did not trace his roots to any Korean master; he went back thousands of years to Śākyamuni Buddha as the source.

It is imperative to understand that the Founding Master unified both: Il-Won-Sang Truth to which he himself awakened, and the Dharmakāya Buddha realized and elucidated by Śākyamuni Buddha, making it clear that the original guide was the Buddha.

"... by modeling ourselves on Il-Won-Sang, the Dharmakāya Buddha"

"... modeling ourselves ..." means adopting an object of faith and a standard for practice. Average people live according to their desires, whatever those may be. A somewhat more advanced person learns from books and family tradition, adopting those as standards for living.

A wiser person turns to a doctrine based on Truth and adopts its teachings as a standard. How about you? Do you look up solely to people and objects? Or do you look up to the Truth?

What does a buddha regard as a standard in life? A buddha adopts Truth as a standard. It was Truth that created the Buddha. We can only hope to become one with Truth if we consciously work to mirror it as the standard of our own practice.

Of course, even those who merely come into contact with Won Buddhism regularly will unwittingly very slowly come to mirror it. But that would take too much time. We need to consciously make up our minds and strive to become one with it. This is the only effective means of doing so. It is of paramount importance.

Modeling ourselves after the Dharmakāya Buddha, Il-Won-Sang Truth does not mean resembling it without any effort on our part. It means setting a standard and dedicating ourselves to becoming one with the Truth.

There are images of the Buddha carrying other buddhas on his head. In other words, the Buddha lives with buddhas on his head so that he might remain one with the mind of the buddhas who achieved enlightenment.

Once we come to carry our teachers on our heads, hold them to our breast, and make active efforts to emulate them, we will discover the unseen mind-Truth as Truth, adopt it as our standard, and become one with it.

CHAPTER 5

THE LIFE OF BECOMING
A BUDDHA THROUGH
THE THREEFOLD PRACTIC

"... vow to practice wholeheartedly to cultivate our minds and bodies perfectly; to know human affairs and universal principles perfectly and to use our minds and bodies perfectly ..."

Children learn implicitly from the actions of their parents. All sages of the three time periods awakened to the Truth of the universe and, believing in that Truth, adopted it as their teacher. The process of awakening to the Truth and instilling it into our minds and bodies is called "practice based on Truth," or "mind practice."

In this chapter, I present a detailed method for instilling Truth into our minds and bodies. Each of us has a unique character. These teachings will guide us to the comprehension of Truth, so it settles into our character and stirs us to discipline ourselves. I hope you will consider the material in this chapter regarding your own character.

"... vow to practice wholeheartedly to cultivate our minds and bodies perfectly ..."

This passage urges us to practice keeping our minds and bodies perfect and faultless when we use them—in other words, to practice cultivation so that we may maintain a healthy body and a mind in its true original mind state. This passage tells us to guard our original mind.

This realm of the original mind refers to a mind state that is ever-calm and ever-alert. The Il-Won-Sang Vow tells us that Il-Won-Sang Truth is the realm of Samādhi beyond words and speech and the Gateway of Birth and Death that transcends Being and Nonbeing. Here, "realm of Samādhi" and "Gateway of Birth and Death" refer to an ever-calm and ever-alert mind.

In "The Dharma of Timeless Zen," the Founding Master called this mind "true emptiness and marvelous existence." He explained that while we have One Mind, it has two aspects: the mind of true emptiness and the mind of marvelous existence.

Depending on the situation, the mind can also be classified into three types of minds. In "The Essential Dharmas of Daily Practice," it is said that the mind is originally free from disturbance, delusion, and wrongdoing. The Scripture of the Founding Master refers to an empty mind, a complete mind, and a right mind.

Whether he is speaking of two minds or three, he is referring to the same One Mind.

The pure original mind that all of us possess is something that we lose in the course of our lives. The original mind becomes tainted, obscured by desire, and skewed by attachment and greed—it becomes shrouded in dark clouds and fog.

When we fly in an airplane, we travel through the clouds before breaking through to see blue sky stretching out endlessly around us. Our sentient being minds are constantly obscured by clouds. Since we can experience neither pleasure nor wisdom when our minds are obscured, this passage tells us to recover the original mind of true emptiness and marvelous existence, our ever-calm and ever-alert mind, whenever and wherever we are.

The person who has awakened to the original mind of Truth will work hard to preserve Truth. Nothing matters more than guarding our minds and bodies so that we have a pure mind. For, even if we do nothing, temptation will enter from outside and build a house in our minds, beckoning us to live within.

Everyone has preconceptions. We build mind houses—houses of the people we love, houses of the people we hate—and we are forever afflicted by them. We become slaves to our preconceptions and are rendered incapable of escaping their trap. Such preconceptions are called "false notions" and "intruding defilements."

The word "intruding" means that they were not within you originally, that they entered from outside.

Because we are filled with these intruding defilements, our original mind loses its luster, and we lose our sovereignty. Our original nature becomes like a vassal state of intruding defilements, just as Korea was for thirty-six years a vassal state of Japan.

Let us rid ourselves of intruding defilements. Our original mind must gain independence. I am referring here to the practice that protects this original mind. The great task of the practice is to determine how to drive away the dark clouds hanging over our original mind—those skewed, twisted, and noxious weeds of intruding defilements—and return to our original mind.

Beginners who are unskilled at practice—and even those who have engaged in a fair bit of practice—need to practice reciting the Buddha's name, as well as other chants. The meaning of "Na-Mu Ah-Me-Tah-Bul," which is the foremost Won Buddhist Chant, means "to return to our original mind and take refuge in it." When we recite this chant, we are summoning our buddha nature.

Once, there were two practitioners who were devoted to reciting the Buddha's name. They met and talked about their impressions during their practice.

One of them said, "I am nothing but the sound of the Buddha's name."

The other practitioner said, "I am nothing but the Buddha's name."

Authentication of having reached a high state, it is said, was given to the practitioner who said that he was merely the Buddha's name, devoid even of the sound of the recitation.

In Won Buddhism, the recitation of the Buddha's name is performed to recover the buddha in our original mind. There is also the Seongju, the "Sacred Chant," which we chant to prepare for the next life or to ask for deliverance of the spirit. When we make a wish, we chant the Yeongju, the "Spiritual Chant." And we chant the Cheongjeongju, the "Purification Chant," when we wish to drive away perverse demons and evil spirits.

If we work hard to learn these chants and we produce the appropriate sounds, the invocations will permeate our minds. This could also provide an occasion for other sentient beings who hear these chants to achieve salvation. Through the merits of the incantation, the intruders of our mind and the dark clouds of the five desires will be stripped away layer by layer. In this way, we will take another step toward recovering our original mind.

Next, there is practice for equanimity of the mind at rest. It is most important to practice calming our mind to equanimity. This is achieved through seated meditation, in the mornings and evenings, and even during the day when we have no work to do. Master Daesan called this "practice to subdue the mind." We work to calm an excited mind until it is serene.

During dharma gatherings, when we strike the bamboo clapper

and say, "Let us enter Samādhi," what happens to our mind? At first, it does not linger even for a short period in Samādhi. It never rests—it buzzes instead with countless thoughts, going back and forth. Indeed, it is even more clamorous than before we were called to enter Samādhi.

But when we breathe appropriately—settling our mind on the breath, settling our mind on the elixir field, settling our mind on gentle music, or quietly settling on an object of focus—the scattered thoughts disappear. Of course, this does not happen in the space of just one or two days. We practice and practice settling the mind on one point, whichever point we choose, so that it becomes a single thought. The single thought deepens until it becomes no-mind.

If we practice like this with dedication, we will learn to open and close the door of our mind. When we can finally shut it tight, we develop the ability to recover our tranquil original nature.

Next, is practice to preserve our original nature during our work. The Founding Master called this practice "Choice in Action" with sound thought. Previously, I talked about practicing to preserve our original nature mainly when we are at rest. When we engage in practice to preserve our original nature during work, we focus single mindedly on what we are doing. This allows us to work efficiently without separation from our original nature.

When average people work, they are usually thinking about something else, so they experience scattered thoughts, greed, and fixation. For this reason, they meet with failure, create negative karma, or develop bad habits. But a practitioner learns to work without leaving the realm of the original mind—continuing to practice during work. This is called "Samādhi in Action."

Few works of brush calligraphy by the Founding Master survive. Yet, there exists one consisting of Chinese characters that read, "Samādhi at Rest, Samādhi in Action" (一相三昧 一行三昧)."

"Samādhi at Rest" means "Truth remains intact during the practice we engage in when at rest." In other words, an ever-calm, ever-alert aspect of the mind prevails. "Samādhi in Action" refers to preserving our ever-calm and ever-alert original mind when at work.

There are other expressions, "Samādhi while reading," or "total immersion in reading." "Samādhi in Action" is also used to refer to the practice of achieving one pointedness of mind during work. This, too, is a form of practice in which we create no-mind during whatever work we are doing without separating from our original mind. It is a method of practice to guard our mind.

Among the dharma instructions by Master Chŏngsan passed down to his students, we find the words, "Practicing no-mind at the onset of every thought is the practice we engage in when we are not working. Taking care of matters joyfully in everything we do is the practice we engage in while at work. If we can engage in thoughtful practice and practice no-mind according to our will, we will acquire great virtue and our mind will grow ever vaster, so there will be no obstructions in anything we do." What this instruction tells us is that we need to engage in the great and perfect practice of One Suchness in both action and rest, in a continuous way.

Among the Zen traditions, we find Tathāgata Zen and Patriarch Zen. Tathāgata Zen is the first of two levels of enlightenment, where we realize the Truth of emptiness as our original nature. Patriarch Zen refers to the second level of enlightenment where we realize the Truth of marvelous existence based on the empty nature of all phenomena. Tathāgata Zen could be said to be the practice of "Samādhi at Rest." Patriarch Zen could be said to be the practice of "Samādhi in Action."

We can only become truly enlightened when we maintain the same mind in action and rest, and it can only be said to be Tathāgata practice when we practice obtaining and using One Mind.

So far, I have been discussing the practice to maintain a tranquil mind in action and rest. But it is also to cultivate the body. We need to cultivate our temperament, which resides in our body. Our minds cannot be properly gathered when our bodies are weak.

The body that I have in this life is the result of the karmic affinities I created with my parents in previous lives. So it is that my body contains a particular consciousness, which we tend to call "I." The body is a house for the "I," a vessel in which it is contained. This consciousness is our temperament.

If the house of the "I" is feeble or flawed, that consciousness will inevitably be affected as it reacts to its environment and to other people, resulting in suffering and uneasiness. The main actor—the one called "I"—must effectively manage the body in which it dwells with a practicing mind. The question is, what do we need to do to preserve the integrity of all the functions that the body possesses?

The Founding Master called the practice to guard the body "external cultivation of the mind,"—it is the cultivation of the mind when dealing with external situations. If we can manage our bodies properly, we have won half the battle in our practice.

Then, we also need to guard the body at the physical level. When you go to a mechanic's garage, you see the words, "Wipe it, tighten it, oil it." So it is with our bodies. We need to wash ourselves clean for the blood to circulate properly. We need to supply ourselves with the right nutrients, which is like oiling the engine. And when necessary, we need to take medicine. If we are meticulous about doing all this, both the cultivation of temperament and the cultivation of mind will proceed in good order, and our practice will guard both mind and body perfectly. This is something that we truly must do constantly—today, tomorrow, and every day through old age, until we die.

The sages said many things about the mind, but little about the body. For all our body's functions to work properly, let us wash our bodies well, give them rest, exercise appropriately, and eat properly. This training of the body is called "external cultivation".

No matter how much courage we may possess in our minds, if our body's energy is weak, we are oppressed by any sensory condition that comes our way and fear occupies our minds. Once in the grip of fear, our minds become clamorous, and we end up making mistakes. This is why discipline of the temperament, or external cultivation of the mind, is so important. If each of us manages our health properly, we will preserve our body. But there is something that we must be wary of during this process.

The mind must truly become the protagonist and tend to the body properly. If we think only of our physical health and do whatever the body commands, this has the ultimate outcome of ruining the mind. Let us then be clear that tending to the body properly means keeping the mind at peace, attaining buddhahood, and delivering sentient beings.

Average humans and animals use their minds as their body dictates.

Yet, if we practice enough, our body will operate according to the dictates of the mind. The higher an animal's level, the more the mind is capable of governing the body.

We must preserve and tame our body so that it functions appropriately according to the dictates of the true protagonist—the mind. This method of guarding mind and body effectively is called "cultivation of mind and body" practice.

"... to know human affairs and universal principles perfectly..."

When you look at me, you see me with your mind. We all recognize sights and sounds through the workings of the mind. This functioning of the mind we call "prajñā awareness" or "primordial awareness."

In terms of our original mind, we are no different from the Buddha. The difference lies in whether we can gather that mind and use it in exactly the right way. This means that we should use it only when necessary and not use it when unnecessary. We also need to engage in practice to wisely make fast and accurate assessments about universal principles and human affairs, so we can make appropriate use of the light of the original mind that we each possess.

When our mind is tranquil, a light emerges within—the light of our original mind. When it is ever-calm, it is also ever-alert. At the beginning of the Il-Won-Sang Vow it is said that the realm of Samādhi is beyond words and speech. When we are in the state of Samādhi, the functional aspect of the Gateway of Birth and Death that transcends Being and Nonbeing is also present.

Our original mind is both true emptiness and marvelous existence. The Dharma of Timeless Zen tells us that when we are in the true emptiness of our original mind, the light of the marvelous existence is also there. In his foundational Daoist book Nanhuajing Zhuangz uses the expression "xushi shengbai." Xushi means "empty room." Taken together, the words mean, "Brightness emerges from an empty room."

Long ago, there was a monk who saw a group of monkeys playing. Quietly, he said to the monk next to him that each of the monkeys was playing with its own ancient mirror. The other monk responded by asking, "How can you sully something that has no name by calling it 'ancient mirror'?"

Here, "ancient mirror" refers to the fundamental awareness present within all of us. Ancient means timeless—no beginning and no end. The monk's reply points to the inadequacy of likening our original mind to a mirror, for it cannot be described by any concept or image.

The Founding Master spoke of the consciousness of Heaven and Earth. Because Heaven and Earth have consciousness, he said, we reap soybeans when we plant soybeans, and we reap red beans when we plant red beans. It is this all-pervading consciousness of Heaven and Earth that is the light of Truth, the inner light that is always with us.

The key to inquiry into human affairs and universal principles is to tend carefully to the sound thought present within all of us. This means that we must learn and awaken to the dharma of using that inner light. Once we have understood and awakened to this, we will be wise people, we will achieve the Status of the Greatly Enlightened Tathāgata, and we will attain buddhahood.

It is human affairs and universal principles that we must understand with our foundational mind and heart—what is right and wrong, what brings benefit and what brings harm.

PRACTICE FOR UNDERSTANDING AND AWAKENING TO HUMAN AFFAIRS

In our human life, we begin to work early in life, and many of us continue working for most of our lives. The person who understands the work ethic well is said to be wise, while the person who does not know how to work is considered incompetent.

Among the many varieties of work, there is edification, the work of transmitting the dharma of the Buddha. The Won Buddhism order was created to carry out this work, and it has since been dedicated to its service. The government, on the other hand, engages in "government business," seeking the welfare of the people and the development of the nation.

Within the home, there is family work. Individuals also engage in their own work—large and small work, highly worthy work and less worthy work, work to be done now, work for the future—the varieties are limitless.

The people who understand work and carry it out effectively and the people who do not understand work and carry it out poorly come together to form societies. When we study the scriptures, when we seek mastery of The Way, our ultimate goal is to work well.

The Founding Master said that we must clearly discern between all the different types of work and their relationship to human affairs in daily life—determining which are correct, which are amiss, which are beneficial, and which are harmful—so that we can handle our work in a way that is correct and beneficial. Average people and sentient beings, however, engage more often in what is improper and harmful, unconsciously helping to make the world a noisy and unfortunate place.

Once, I happened to attend a trial at Jeonju District Court. The defendant was a public servant who played cards on Sundays. The prosecutor contended that the man had gambled with public money that he carried in his pocket, and that he should be sternly punished. This was around the time of the coup on May 16, 1961. The prosecutor harshly criticized the defendant and recommended an especially heavy sentence because he had conducted himself in a way unbefitting the status of public servant at a time when the nation needed to establish discipline.

Sitting in the courtroom, I truly believed that what the prosecutor said was correct.

Later, the defendant's attorney made his argument. "There isn't a Korean alive who hasn't gotten caught up playing cards," the attorney said. "When you've caught the fever, you gamble your food away, and you gamble your money away, and pretty soon you can end up gambling with the public monies in your pocket. On top of that, he was playing with old friends on Sundays. This was not such a great misdeed. Be lenient with him." Hearing this seasoned attorney's argument, I found myself thinking this could also be true.

I had heard the prosecutor and believed his argument to be plausible. And I had heard the defense attorney and believed that he was not mistaken, either. I imagined the judge would have quite a bit of difficulty making a decision.

Our actions may be well done or poorly done depending on perspective and circumstances, and sometimes poorly done actions are in fact well done actions. It is very difficult to know for sure. But once we engage in proper practice regarding human affairs, we can benefit society and realize success at the individual level at the same time.

PRACTICE TO UNDERSTAND AND AWAKEN TO UNIVERSAL PRINCIPLES

The next thing we need to understand is universal principles. We call this the "Study of Truth." Previously, I spoke about human affairs that are right or wrong, beneficial, or harmful. These are social issues that arise during a human life—things that are personal for each individual.

From the point of view of human affairs as social phenomena, we need to look more deeply into the principles that govern them and examine which actions are right or wrong, beneficial or harmful, as they unfold, according to those principles. We must therefore engage in the study of Truth to understand human affairs fully and precisely, so that we can perform correct and beneficial actions at every level of our lives.

This world contains within it a world of the sentient and a world of the nonsentient. They each operate according to their own principles. We will find that both the inanimate world and the world of living creatures are governed by one great principle. When we have mastered that principle, we will have achieved our goal of understanding universal principles.

The Founding Master calls this single realm the Realm of the Great. This is the realm of the Il-Won-Sang principle.

Truth, in Won Buddhism, is seen as two aspects of one whole. There is the unchanging aspect, or the absolute, called the Realm of the Great, which is emptiness as well as our original nature. Then there is the phenomenological aspect, in which all things arise from that absolute Truth. This changing aspect is called the Realm of the Small. Yet, each of these things that arises and ceases in the Realm of the Small has its own distinctive principles. For instance, water has a cohesive property, while the property of fire is to spread out. In this realm, all things arise and cease. Thoughts and emotions also arise from the mind, whose original nature is emptiness.

Since material things, as well as thoughts and emotions, are constantly arising and ceasing, the Founding Master denominated that changing aspect the "Realm of Being and Nonbeing." There is a hidden principle that operates on those constant changes that keep shifting from Being to Nonbeing and vice versa. When we deal with these ever-changing thoughts and emotions, we need to shine the light of our true nature on them so we can effectively understand the "right and wrong," as well as the "benefit and harm" of human affairs. We will then understand the principles of "Great and Small" and of "Being and Nonbeing," which are the moving force of this universe and of this civilization.

Let me explain the method for achieving this understanding and awakening.

First, let's understand human affairs and universal principles.

We know human affairs and universal principles through our studies and experiences. To understand each of them individually, we need to interact with and learn from teachers or from people who have already experienced them. To this end, we teach and study history, to learn from the experiences of those who have gone before us.

There are forerunners and experienced persons in every type of activity in this world. It is important to learn from them the principles of both Great and Small, as well as "benefit and harm" that are the effect of the choices we make with any act. At the same time, we must understand the principles of "right and wrong" through our own personal experience, so that we can maintain, throughout our lives—regardless of appearances or age—the mind of a student always willing to learn.

As we study the doctrine, we come to understand the standards for determining what is right or wrong, beneficial, or harmful. Throughout history, humans have studied the scriptures set down by sages. Those scriptures create standards for human actions and criteria for determining good and evil.

The studies of the scriptures ultimately provide us with a code of law, as well as social principles, ethics, and morals. In the past, religious teachings were an important element in every society and their study was a means to leadership.

Today, we live in a very different era. Shamans, singers, and performers were disregarded in the past. Now, singers and performers are given the highest regard.

We are currently experiencing a great reversal. While the scriptures of the past were standards for behavior in their time, they are unsuited as standards for behavior for a future time.

We will only become leaders of the future world if we intently study scriptures that present us with new values and modes of behavior for the upcoming age—for we can only apply anything effectively when we repeatedly assess and practice what we have learned.

Next, we must awaken to the universal principles.

We can accumulate a vast store of knowledge by constantly asking questions of a teacher or an enlightened master. But we do not become enlightened through study alone. In order to obtain the high level of wisdom characteristic of a sage and to free ourselves from unwholesome destinies and samsara, we need to achieve our own awakenings through our practice.

Presently, we are engaged in the study of the Il-Won-Sang Vow. We may believe that we are gaining understanding, but once back in our everyday reality, we may easily forget what we have learned, or we may be confused when listening to alternate teachings. No teaching can become totally ours merely through study. We need to personally awaken to it. When we apply in our own lives what we have learned through our dedicated and committed study, we inevitably find ourselves asking questions.

When reality differs from what we have studied, we begin asking questions such as, "Why is this happening?" Once we commit to answering those questions, we experience the truly great joy of awakening when the "aha! moment" inevitably arrives.

As a child, the Founding Master had questions about the sky and the clouds. Also, when he saw his own parents being tender with each other while the couple next door kept fighting, he asked, "Why is that happening?" He harbored profound questions about the universe, nature, and life, so he decided to consult a mountain spirit and a teacher to find the answers. In the end he was unable to find a mountain spirit or to understand the answers of a teacher.

All these questions eventually merged into one big question for him: "What am I to do?" The day he answered that question is the day we recognize as Great Enlightenment and Founding Day. This is the reason why the Founding Master said that questioning is the key to great enlightenment.

As we move forward in our lives, we encounter many things that we cannot understand. Likewise, as we study Won Buddhism we may also find we cannot understand much of what is being said. When we encounter a statement that does not make sense to us, instead of passing it by, we should persist in investigating it further. If we still do not understand it, we should regard it as a critical issue and focus our practice on elucidating it.

Master Daesan said that if a practitioner has no questions in his notebook, he is not a true practitioner. It is important that we identify questions, one at a time, from our everyday life. Profound questions that are not clearly formulated in our minds cannot be answered; they merely make our heads hurt. We must proceed persistently, beginning with the questions that are weighing on our minds right now. When I contrast the things that I fervently believe with reality, the disparity between them sometimes leaves me immersed in profound questions. Questions can also arise out of our deep study of the scriptures. At other times, a teacher may present us with the right question.

If we carry that question with us and we study it intently with a clear mind, we then need to let it go and inquire deeply into it again. If we repeat this process over and over, there will come a time when the fog lifts and we see the path ahead of us.

Once, there was a young minister who went to pay respects to a teacher. "How old are you?" the teacher asked, to which the younger man replied by telling his chronological age.

"No, no," the teacher said. "How old is your mind?" The minister was left speechless, unable to answer. That question—what was the age of his mind—was driven into his heart like a nail, so he thought about the matter deeply and finally became realized.

How about you? How old is your mind? I do not mean your body. Our scriptures contain twenty "Essential Cases for Questioning." If you read them attentively, or if you read the chapters in The Scripture of the Founding Master, you will find questions arising in your mind about the principles.

Once those questions arise, we contemplate them and inquire about them so we can understand them. During our search, we will discover things that we do not understand no matter how much we investigate their meaning. If we incubate them as a hen does an egg, they will reward us with an awakening.

THE PRACTICE OF THE APPRAISAL OF OUR REALIZATIONS

As our practice deepens and we gain enlightenment experiences and understandings, the possibility arises that we may become arrogant. We often witness people who noisily proclaim their realizations to the world.

A few years back, stories about the "rapture" were all over the newspapers. It was said that someone who believed in a particular religion and prayed fervently, would be saved and ascend to Heaven. Many people were shocked when the appointed time for the rapture came and no one ascended to heaven.

Cases like this are not simply about people being taken in by the preposterous claims of a religious leader. Those leaders might have experienced spiritual realizations, but they were mistaken realizations. Among the different types of mistaken realizations, we find misapprehensions, misguided thinking, and misperceptions. If there is a bias in our perceptions, we grasp only one aspect of the realization. In such cases, we awaken only partially but are convinced we have awakened to the whole. Consequently, when we experience an awakening, the first thing to do is to take it to our teacher for appraisal.

Buddhists call this practice "authentication," or "approval of enlightenment." If this process is neglected, we are liable to suffer major frustrations. In the outer world, we are given a certification—a graduation diploma, for example—when we complete the appropriate studies. The purpose of a certification is to guard the process from mistakes.

If there is something we understand for certain in the principles of Great and Small, Being and Nonbeing, right and wrong, benefit and harm, we must put it into practice in our daily life. Once we embody what we have understood and practiced it in depth and breadth within our daily life, we may sense inadequacies in our awakenings. In such cases, we must repeat the process to broaden and deepen our awakenings.

At first, we awaken to the original nature of the mind and to the fact that we and the universe are one. Next, we awaken to how the karmic principle of cause and effect works internally within our mind, and we awaken to the principle of alternating predominance of yin and yang as it works externally in the universe. We then come to the realization that all things are interdependent through cause and effect, and we become capable of predicting how things will unfold in the future based on what we see in the present. This is a process of small realizations that come together to form one great enlightenment.

"... and to cultivate our minds and bodies perfectly ..."

Our bodies and minds are suffused with marvelous creative transformations. Our compassion for someone who is poor, the distress we feel after committing a misdeed, our desire to repay a debt of gratitude, our desire to rest after vigorous exercise and to move again after we rest—all these are the profound workings of Il-Won Truth. When the universe changes through formation, duration, decay and extinction, as well as through spring, summer, autumn and winter, and when all things change through birth, old age, sickness and death—they are all the profound workings of Truth. When Truth operates, it does so in a way suited to each particular time and place. We sentient beings engage in practice with the purpose of using our minds and bodies perfectly by awakening to and becoming one with Il-Won-Sang Truth.

The Founding Master used the term Choice in Action to refer to the practice of using mind and body perfectly. This means that such a practice involves boldly doing that which must be done and boldly abandoning that which must be abandoned. Once we use our minds and bodies properly, blessings and virtue will accumulate, and we will be filled with the happy feeling of ultimate bliss.

Though there may be a realization that comes from gaining the power of cultivation through Cultivating the Spirit, as well as the power of inquiry through the practice of Inquiry, neither of them will produce real effects if we do not put them into practice in our daily lives. Threefold in Action Practice could be called the blossoming, the product, and the goal of the Threefold Practice.

THE NEED TO INSTILL GOOD HABITS

The practice of using the mind and body perfectly involves, first, breaking our bad habits and instilling good ones.

Each of us has certain habits of the mind—habits of resentment, of fancy, of anxiety—the usual habits of sentient beings. These habits ultimately manifest themselves in actions, so we may end up committing misdeeds.

We also have habits of speech. Some people have good minds, but their words may be coarse or unrefined. Habits of speech can cause fissures between us and others, and ultimately breed resentments.

Next, there are habits of the body—the way we move our body. If our habits are unsophisticated, uncultivated, or rude, others may undervalue us.

Let us sincerely commit to uncovering these negative, habitual characteristics of sentient beings in ourselves, and to replacing them with good habits.

"The Essential Dharmas of Daily Practice" is a standard for instilling good habits, while "The Essential Discourse on Commanding Our True Nature" and "The Precepts" provide examples that can lead us to use our mind and bodies using the habits of a buddha-bodhisattva.

Only by practicing proper habits and utterly abandoning improper ones—no matter how comfortable and appealing we may find them—

do we engage in Threefold in Action Practice. All average people and sentient beings possess sentient being habits picked up during their countless previous lives. We call this "personality" or "individuality." But if we have habits that are not helpful for our own development, habits that block the path ahead of us or that go against the moral code of society, we need to ferret each of them out and put our heart and spirit into changing them. Bad habits become instilled without our awareness, and it is very difficult to break them. Yet we do have a choice. Let us break them for our own sake, for our family's sake, and for our community's sake. We develop habits thoughtlessly, thinking little of them, and this becomes a trap for us, preventing us from ever being free. Breaking those bad habits is a shortcut to buddhahood.

Our original mind is tranquil by nature, wise by nature, harmonious and virtuous and righteous by nature. If we wish to make the proper Choices in Action, we need to first recover both the harmony that is the natural aspect of our minds and the precepts inherent in our original mind, and then use a mind that is free of error at every time and in every place.

Il-Won Truth governs this universe. With its limitless power of creative transformations, it functions as a source that propels the universe through changes of formation, duration, decay and extinction. It causes, as well, the succession of spring, summer, autumn, and winter. It governs the changes of birth, old age, sickness, and death. It causes the winds, clouds, rain, dew, frost, and snow, and drives all things to grow and bear fruit according to their characteristics. In the Il-Won-Sang Vow, this is called the Gateway of Birth and Death that transcends Being and Nonbeing.

THE NEED TO PUT OUR REALIZATIONS INTO PRACTICE

In the proper sequence for practice, we first clearly understand human affairs and universal principles with a mind free of delusion and disturbances. Coming to our own understandings before putting something into practice is like creating a blueprint before building a house. If we have a good blueprint, we will build a good house. In everything we do, it is important first to complete our blueprint, and only afterwards begin construction. Proceeding before first arriving at a clear conclusion is an exceedingly foolish and dangerous thing to do. If we first think clearly about whatever we are going to do in our immediate reality and then put it into practice with the correct use of mind and body, we are practicing what we call Choice in Action, which is free of error. Yet, in many cases our understandings may be unclear or incomplete, in which case we behave according to habit or circumstance. That is why we need to make sure we have a precise understanding of the principles before we put them into practice.

Some people who are born with a higher spiritual level and capabilities—likely acquired through practice in previous lives—may experience what is termed "sudden enlightenment."

For example, someone who is walking may come across a muddy stream and, by just looking at it, suddenly understands the inner workings of the universe—this is called "sudden enlightenment." If this complete understanding is put into practice without hesitation—this is called "sudden cultivation."

Those who are still unskilled with their practice need to work hard when using mind and body to engage in inquiry into human affairs and universal principles. Then they need to verify their understanding and use it as a kind of compass or blueprint for their practice. When we understand something but fail to put it into practice due to old habits or excessive desire, it is as if we are issuing a check with insufficient funds.

The Founding Master instructed us to do what we know is right even at the risk of our lives. Yet, average people seem to keep their understandings and practice separate. We need to arrive at understandings that are possible to be put into practice, and once we have formed them we must have the will to practice them.

In our interactions with people, we find some who show clear thinking but are incapable of putting their thoughts into practice when confronted with reality. Such persons are "idea persons." In a sense, those persons are like a beautiful plant that fails to bloom. But such persons can gradually come to achieve realistic goals if they commit themselves fully to putting their understandings into practice.

THE NEED TO USE MIND AND BODY ACCORDING TO CIRCUMSTANCES

Even when we come to a right understanding, the possibility exists that the circumstances will be different on the ground, so we might need to modify the understanding we achieved and form a new one. In such cases, it could be said that the choice goes to a higher level, for it is important that our practice be suited to the circumstances of each time and place, regardless of any ideas we may have had beforehand. This is called "Middle Way Practice."

The most effective form of action is the appropriate use of body and mind in a way suited to the circumstances of each time and place. This could be termed "flexible practice."

Consider a football match. The first thing the coach does is to examine the opposing team's tactical plan. He then establishes his own plan and trains the athletes to follow his tactics. Even so, the other team's plan may be different once the match begins, in which case it becomes necessary to shift rapidly away from the planned tactics.

If the car we are driving jerks at every start and stop, people may think we do not know how to drive. When someone is a good driver, we do not notice when that person starts or stops. In the same way, a higher level of Choice in Action only emerges when we engage in actions while mindfully and seamlessly removing all hesitations to achieve Choice in Action.

Once we have gained enough practice with Choice in Action, our heart and mind reach coherence, a state of harmony that gives us the power to regulate our energy as we wish. Once we can regulate our own energy, we gain the ability to regulate the energy of other people. If we work constantly to change our habits of mind and body, put our understandings into practice, and engage in Middle Way Practice suited to each time and place, we become one with Truth. The cornerstone of Threefold in Action Practice is our capacity to assess our states of mindfulness and unmindfulness. I believe that it is only possible for someone to become a sage after practicing mindfulness hundreds of millions of times.

What enables us to change our habits, put our thoughts into practice, and engage in Choice and Action is the cultivation of the spirit. This is what we call "mindfulness practice."

Changes in Heaven and Earth proceed naturally and automatically. I referred to this above as the "Gateway of Birth and Death that transcends Being and Nonbeing." In the Gateway our mind rises when we encounter a sensory condition, and it changes to a different kind of mind or disappears completely when the condition ceases.

Thoughts change according to a process of arising, enduring, transforming, and ceasing. The mind changes based on this process, and nature becomes the Gateway of Birth and Death naturally and automatically. Yet, it is impossible to open and close the Gateway of Birth and Death in our mind simply according to our wishes. To make that happen, it is crucial that we train ourselves and engage in Threefold in Action Practice to command the opening and closing of our mind.

We are capable of thinking and not thinking. The Gateway of the mind can be adjusted like the aperture of a camera. When we reach the point where we can do this effortlessly, dharma power emerges within us, we become sages, and we are able to unite with the universe.

Those who have chosen the path of practice, close the doors of their minds tightly so no thought can enter, and they open and close their minds, so their inner thoughts do not escape to the outside. This is what we call the mind's Choice in Action. We train our mind to assess when we are mindful or unmindful—this is the foundation of Threefold in Action Practice.

When we use mind and body properly, we can use our minds as we wish and use our bodies as we will. Sentient beings are tormented by their bodies. They suffer because they are unable to control the desires that arise in their minds. Then both body and mind become places of torment.

But if we cultivate The Way properly and use body and mind well, we create ultimate bliss in our mind and we create a paradise in our bodies, then the body becomes a good house for the spirit.

When body and mind are used properly, they become instruments for the creation of blessings. As a result, we bring peace to the world and create eternal lives for ourselves, filled with abundant blessings and wisdom.

Previously, we considered methods for engaging in the practices of Cultivating the Spirit, Inquiry into human affairs and universal principles, and Choice in Action. We can observe people who focus primarily on Cultivating the Spirit and engage only in a practice that will give them an impression of stability and purity. Others focus on Inquiry and possess only knowledge or wisdom. Still others focus on Choice in Action, so only their capabilities and know-how are strong. When someone focuses on only one aspect of the practice, character flaws will emerge. Just as we develop malnutrition and sicken if we do not have a balanced diet, it is misguided for us to focus on only one area of mind practice or to believe that any one area is more important than the others.

Il-Won-Sang Truth has three aspects: an empty and calm aspect, a luminous aspect, and a creative transformations aspect. Let us incorporate all these aspects perfectly into our practice. If we incorporate only one element of Il-Won-Sang, we will not truly understand Il-Won-Sang Truth. Instead, we would be like a child who thinks only of his father and ignores the cares of his mother.

The Founding Master was wary of the practitioner who would engage only in cultivation and neglect practice, engage only in inquiry, and lack cultivation, or while being deficient in his inquiry, put his understanding into practice. He said that such a person was "only partially a person of The Way" and cautioned us about that highly mistaken form of practice. We need to carry out all three elements of the Threefold Practice (Cultivation, Inquiry, and Choice) so that we may become imbued with a character that is perfect, like Il-Won-Sang.

CHAPTER 6

THE LIFE OF PROGRESSION AND GRACE

"...progressing rather than regressing and receiving grace rather than harm..."

The meaning of this part of the Vow is that we should regard the Dharmakāya Buddha, Il-Won-Sang as the object of our faith and the model of our practice, and commit ourselves to our faith on the Dharmakāya Buddha, Fourfold Grace and to the Threefold Practice with utmost devotion, so that our character and dharma stage progress. It means that as we receive blessings from the Fourfold Grace, we should not allow our character and dharma stage to regress, that we must cultivate our buddha nature by ensuring that we do are not reciprocated with harm from the Fourfold Grace, that we should tame our bodies and our actions to create a life that is a constant source of grace in our relationships with others—so we do not receive harm from them.

"...to practice wholeheartedly..."
There is nothing more important in our lives than sincerity. Sincere dedication means constant repetition, with sound thought. Only when we have achieved all these qualities—authentic dedication, zeal, right values and constant repetition—will we have attained wholehearted practice.

A student once asked his teacher, "What is the single most important word in this world?" Immediately, the teacher responded by writing the word "sincerity." "'Sincerity' is the most important word," the teacher said. "Commit yourself sincerely to everything you do."

The *Doctrine of the Mean*, a well-known Chinese classic, says, "Without sincerity and dedication, there is nothing." Without sincere dedication, nothing can exist and no ventures can succeed.

If we are to dedicate ourselves sincerely, we must have a standard. Without a standard, there can be no true commitment, and our sincerity will not be sustained.

That standard is our faith in Il-Won-Sang and the Threefold Practice. We must adopt four standards—one for requiting the Fourfold Grace, one for Cultivating the Spirit, one for Inquiry into human affairs and universal principles, and one for Choice in Action.

Every one of us has had the experience of making a firm resolution, only to see it last a mere three days. Sincere commitment means repeating those three-days resolutions again and again, stringing them together until they last a lifetime. In other words, we need to engage in constant repetition based on a standard.

It is said that a heavyweight boxer has the power of a four-ton truck in his fists. The release of such power from such a small fist is possible from repeated practice.

Through the Threefold Practice we can generate the same kind of power by means of constant repetition of our actions based on our original mind, which is bright, clear and compassionate. Even with constant repetition, there will be no great effect if we do so without mindfulness or while thinking other thoughts. We need to engage in repetition with One Mind. When we are sincere in our commitment, we gain strength and awesome power.

We feel something magical when we see a practitioner of Chinese medicine at work. Although the dosage is written on the prescription, even when the practitioner merely picks it up with his fingers without weighing it on the scale, it is exactly the right weight.

An intuitive knowledge grows over the course of constant repetitions. Our mothers, too, could apply a dash of salt while preparing our meals to produce exactly the right degree of saltiness. This is all the result of sincere commitment.

If you pray wholeheartedly and commit to the Threefold Practice with utmost sincerity, you will gradually acquire the ability to see into the future. You will also develop inner mental powers and outward powers of influence, which will allow you to leave deep impressions on others.

Typically, we dedicate ourselves sincerely only to those things we experience through our senses. How important is it, then, to realize that if we begin to give our sincere commitment to a mind that is unseen and unknowable—to Il-Won-Sang Truth that governs the universe—the awesome powers that result will be far greater and will come much faster.

THE LIFE OF PROGRESSION

"Progression" means that if we sincerely commit ourselves to faith and practice, our character and dharma power will grow.

If we engage in the Threefold Practice, we will be reborn with a character of freedom, wisdom, and mercy. Our life will be transformed from an empty life obscured by desires into a life of Truth—we will become sages. This is what is meant by progression.

People live a variety of lifestyles within their different societies. Some live worthwhile lives while some do not.

Those living the lives of denizens of hell wander hopelessly amid sickness and pain. To such people, the delivering hand of a sage is far away indeed. Those who fixate solely on eating, like hungry ghosts, or on combativeness, give no consideration to ethics, morality, or to any thing or person other than themselves.

Those living the lives of animals give themselves over to a filthy and dissolute life without manners or shame, indulging in carnal desires and indolence. Others live the lives of asuras: ever roaming and without order, lacking any center in what they do, without any direction.

Those living the lives of human beings have either desirous minds or virtuous minds. They alternate between joy and pain and entertain either the mind of The Way or an unwholesome mind, depending on circumstances. Among human beings, we find those of the uppermost stratum who are fully aware and live a conscious life. This is the class of buddha-bodhisattvas—practitioners of The Way who live heavenly lives, experience simple desires, enjoy performing acts of generosity, live according to the mind of The Way and never fail to engage in deep reflection. Of course, if a human being adopts the mind of one of the other five destinies for too long, the habits and dharma power from this lifetime may result in regression in the next. The human being who adopts the habits of a denizen of hell may be born in an actual hell, while the person who adopts the habits of the asura may fail to receive a body and instead roam about as a ghost.

As stated above, when we commit ourselves sincerely to a life of faith and cultivation of The Way, we will progress from an animal's life to a human being's life, or from a human being's life to a heavenly being's life.

There was once a Won Buddhist who was living the life of a hungry ghost. So severe was it that he was ostracized from his home and neighborhood for being a good-for-nothing. But after a decade or so of Won Buddhism mind practice, which he entered thanks to a karmic affinity with a minister, the change was so great that other believers and the people in his neighborhood lauded him as having become an enlightened one. Of course, we will still have to wait and see, but it may be the case that he progressed several levels, from asura to heavenly being.

Among the practitioners at the Elementary Stage who take refuge in Won Buddhism, become members, and receive dharma names, we find people at every stage imaginable. There are those who have lived the lives of denizens of hell, those who have been requited with the asura destiny and lived a life of roaming, and those who have always enjoyed the heavenly bliss of an enlightened one living a complete life.

If these practitioners from different stages carry out the four duties—morning and evening prayer, helping others, observance of regulations, and guiding other people to buddhadharma—and if they engage in mind practice for many decades, they will ultimately progress to the Special Faith Stage, the Battle Between Dharma and Māra Stage, the Dharma Strong and Māra Defeated Stage, the Beyond the Household Stage, and the Highly Enlightened Tathāgata Stage.

Imagine what a great life these average human beings, who are cycling through the six destinies, will lead once they meet a great teacher and progress to the level of buddha-bodhisattva. They will then freely take charge of the six destinies and be able to choose how and where they are born.

Whenever I develop a lazy mind during my practice or I begin to feel resentful of others, I repeat the words of one of our hymns: "It is difficult to become a human, yet I have already become one. It is difficult to hear the buddhadharma, yet I am already hearing it. If my body cannot be delivered in this life, then what life must I wait for to be delivered?" When I do so, I experience my mind coming to life, and a mind of dedication arises. Let us all dedicate ourselves with zeal and accumulate good works so we can proceed along the path of progression.

THE LIFE OF REGRESSION

Regression happens when our humanity deteriorates, when we go astray—when our faith and our practice lapse for extended periods of time.

Sometimes, even if filled with faith and dedication in our Won Buddhism practice, our environment suddenly improves or deteriorates, and we let go of our practice and our generous deeds. When this happens, we end up regressing.

At other times, while in the Battle Between the Dharma and Māra Stage, we gain understanding or are recognized by others, so we may develop a feeling of arrogance. Then we come to think lightly of our teacher or minister. When this happens, our mind is gradually corrupted, laziness emerges, and we regress.

It is said that when we go astray after engaging in the Battle Between the Dharma and Māra, it becomes ever more difficult to achieve enlightenment. We may find ourselves blaming others for our regression in our workplace or family circumstances. At that point it is most important to understand that problems of our mind and self are far more powerful than any outer influence.

In order to avoid regression, let us establish a firm faith, for the greatest cause of regression is a weak faith. The next greatest cause is greed. All things grow through gradual changes according to a sequence—the same is true for practice and faith. They proceed from small to large. When we practice and act with a spirit of greed, we become impatient, and if things fail to live up to our hopes, we feel frustrated and give up, so we end up regressing.

The next thing we must be wary of is laziness. We are all given to indolence, to seeking comfort. Our bodies have an ever-present desire for comfort. Cultivation of The Way demands a sincere commitment—if we allow ourselves to be hindered by indolence and we keep putting things off until the next day, we will wind up a perennial regressor.

We must be wary of delusion. Living an effective life of faith and cultivation of The Way requires wisdom. If we pursue The Way foolishly, without any knowledge, we end up regressing.

At school, we find people who fail to graduate and must repeat a year, in which case, they may experience shame. If people who are wealthy and used to traveling everywhere by taxi suddenly lose all their money and are forced to walk instead, they may find it difficult to bear.

But while the person who strives even after regressing can rise once again, the person who has given up and hopelessly resigned himself to regression will go from regression to regression, and from hardship to greater hardship. It is a truly sad sight to behold.

In Bojo's article *Secrets on Cultivating the Mind,*, it says that an average person encountering buddhadharma is like a blind turtle encountering a piece of driftwood. To survive out in the ocean, a blind turtle needs to find a branch to sit on and breathe. But it is not easy to find drifting branches in a vast ocean, and even if one happens to float by, it is very difficult for a blind turtle to climb on it.

But all of you here have found this true dharma. Believe in it wholeheartedly, devote yourselves to your teachers' teachings, learn from them, and practice on your own. In this way, you will progress rather than regress.

"... receiving grace ..."

When we act, we necessarily affect other people and objects either directly or indirectly. If our influence is positive, the fruits of grace will be delivered to us. If our influence is negative, we will reap the fruits of harm from others in the future. If we are mindful to make buddha offerings to everyone we encounter, we will ensure we receive grace.

When are facing trying times, when we are having difficulty making a decision, when our minds are restless and obscured by desire, when we have become arrogant about things we have done well, we must put our palms together before the Dharmakāya Buddha and offer a prayer. And if we abide by the precepts, empty our minds through seated meditation practice and timeless Zen practice, awaken to cause and effect by studying the scriptures every chance we get, open our eyes to the principle of Our true nature, and engage in many years of the Threefold Practice to become aware of human affairs, we will continually progress as individuals.

The progressing person naturally gives off a bright, clear, and warm energy all around. When we follow a life of prayer, an auspicious energy will be transmitted to the karmic affinities around us that will even spread on to the affinities of those affinities.

Just as television is broadcast and telephone calls are transmitted through wavelengths of electricity, so a wavelength of grace propagates from the person who is progressing. The hidden help and hidden virtue of the Dharmakāya Buddha, Fourfold Grace opens the Gateway of grace ahead of the progressing person. This is due in part to the earnest attention of the person's teachers.

Average people do not know who is giving them blessings and happiness. They have a vague belief that it is the result of good luck or the stars, or perhaps their ancestors. The lives of average people are full of contradictions—it could be said that they are living unsatisfactory lives, merely wishing for a stroke of good fortune.

Everyone has a personal destiny and a variety of past lives. Sometimes, seemingly unanticipated blessings and happiness occur, and sometimes ill fortune appears unexpectedly. What exactly is providing these blessings, this happiness, these catastrophes?

Only when we understand with certainty the deeper factors that drive these events can we be said to have acquired the wisdom of Truth. The disasters that befall us and the blessings and happiness that come our way are not the result of our having tended the ancestral gravesite well or inadequately, nor do they result from our having a propitious or a dubious site for our home. Nor indeed do they come from an unfair god who deals blessings to some and disaster to others.

As is explained at the very beginning of the Il-Won-Sang Vow,

Il-Won-Sang Truth is the realm that transcends Being and Nonbeing. It is beyond all issues of like and dislike. It delivers misfortunes or blessings depending exclusively on the effects that each of us has caused, according to our mental and bodily functioning.

This is why we talk about receiving what we create for ourselves. If we do good to others, Il-Won-Sang Truth gives us blessings and happiness, and if we do harm to others the Il-Won-Sang Truth Buddha will not fail to bring us harm.

When we give something to somebody, that person gives back to us. We do not give to the person in the south and receive from the person in the north. We need to act from a firm belief in the principle of reaping as we sow and work diligently to accumulate acts of generosity for all people and all living creatures around us. Most important is to act from our deepening understanding of Il-Won-Sang Truth. This will naturally cause us to act with goodwill towards everyone and everything around us, and we will reap the same rewards.

Those acts of generosity create the blessings we receive in this life or the next. Let us awaken to the karmic principle of cause and effect, knowing that we reap as we sow with every individual. Let us understand what each person needs and how we can help them progress and generate grace effectively by performing a buddha offering suited to each of them.

If any person we have helped in this life commits a misdeed against us, let us accept it as requital for a debt from a previous life. Yet, if we continue to help this person, the harm will be converted to grace.

We are familiar with the figure of the Zen Patriarch Huineng. One evening, he was trying to go to sleep, when he perceived a strange lust for blood. In deep contemplation of his affairs in the past, he realized that he had failed to repay a debt of ten lings of silver in a past life. He then became acutely aware that someone was coming to reclaim the debt. Huineng left the ten lings of silver under his mat and hid where he could watch. When the perpetrator came, Huineng saw that it was another monk named Xingchang.

Huineng came out of hiding and said, "I failed to repay a debt of ten lings of silver to you in a previous life, but that is not worth blood in your hand. Take the coins and go."

After that, the story goes, Xingchang reflected deeply and became immensely grateful before finally becoming a special student of Huineng.

Fundamentally, if we gain the three great powers of the Threefold Practice, possess a warm virtuousness in our hearts and remain constant in our dedication to serve others, our words and deeds will ever be those of generous mercy in both mind and body. But our acts of generosity and merit will only be great—will only become eternal grace—when we perform them without any indication that we have done so.

"... rather than harm ..."

The person who is regressing will begin to be treated poorly and even scornfully and will receive little or no aid from neighbors, colleagues and acquaintances. Harm is the misfortune that seemingly "happens to come our way." Yet, it is the natural byproduct of cause and effect. By nature, Heaven and Earth, our parents, our fellow beings, and laws afford us unlimited grace. But although the progressing person simply receives this grace, the regressing or ungrateful person receives grace as harm.

When we were children, things like honey and taffy were delicious treats. The progressing person has self-control and can measure the effects of the honey and consume it in appropriate amounts for its health benefits.

The regressing person lacks self-control and may, for example, eat it indiscriminately with little understanding of the positive uses of honey. Honey affords the same sweet grace to the progressing person and the regressing person alike. Yet, the progressing person uses it graciously, in a healthy way, while the regressing person uses it to excess and may receive harm.

All beings are imbued with a unique energy, depending on the way their minds function. When that energy is strong, it transforms into a wave that ripples out to the people around them. Those who are progressing generally send out waves of grace, causing a beneficial ripple effect in other people and organizations. The people and objects that encounter these waves of grace respond in kind with their own waves of grace.

A person who is progressing receives grace. In contrast, a person who is regressing, has constant desires to harm others, and naturally comes to project waves of harm to both individuals and groups. When this happens, the person becomes isolated. Those who received the waves of harm will eventually retaliate. The regressing person will always receive retribution and will go from pain to suffering.

Our six sense organs (eyes, ears, nose, tongue, body, and mind) can be instruments for creating grace or instruments for creating harm.

Our faith and practice will turn those organs into instruments for creating grace. This is dedication and Zen.

If we use our sense organs to make buddha offerings to others that produce grace, it stands to reason that grace will return to us. Conversely, if we choose to use those precious instruments of our body and our mind in a way that creates harm—whether out of greed, fixation, or bad habit—those who experience that harm, unless they are buddhas, will inevitably respond in kind with harm. This requital is a creative transformation belonging to the Gateway of Birth and Death that transcends Being and Nonbeing.

Fortunately, we have learned the path of progression, and we have learned to drive back regression. Let us remain awake and resolve to create grace with our six sense organs, and not inflict misfortune and regression upon ourselves by producing harm.

CHAPTER 7

THE RESULT OF COMPLETING OUR VOW

"...we unawakened beings vow to practice wholeheartedly to cultivate our minds and bodies perfectly; to know human affairs and universal principles perfectly and to use our minds and bodies perfectly, thus progressing rather than regressing and receiving grace rather than harm, until we attain the awesome power of Il-Won and become one with the nature of Il-Won."

When we make a vow to attain the limitless, awesome power of Il-Won-Sang Truth and to put this vow into practice, and when we make a vow to become Il-Won-Sang Truth and put that into practice, we become a Tathāgata—we achieve the great, perfect and right enlightenment. That is the completion of our vow.

Attaining the awesome power of Il-Won and becoming one with its substance and nature delivers the state of a buddha who has experienced the great enlightenment of the Dharmakāya Buddha, Il-Won-Sang Truth. This is the status of the Tathāgatas who, having made Il-Won-Sang Truth completely their own, have attained the power of the Fourfold Grace.

As we progress and continue progressing even further, eventually we become one with the substance and nature of Il-Won-Sang. As we receive grace and continue receiving grace, we attain the awesome power of Il-Won-Sang. This is called the ultimate vow—a vow through which Il-Won-Sang becomes our own.

"... attain the awesome power of Il-Won..."

The universe is truly vast, Heaven and Earth truly eternal. There is an entity that governs Heaven and Earth. It is called Il-Won-Sang

Truth.

This Truth delivers myriad creative transformations and awesome power. It has the power to transform the universe through formation, duration, decay, and extinction. It also has the power to give forth the limitless creative transformations, and the power to deliver the progression or regression to all living creatures through birth, old age, sickness, and death, according to their mental and bodily functioning in the four types of birth.

How much does this Earth weigh? How heavy is the moon? The massive moon circles the Earth once every month. The Earth revolves on its own axis while also orbiting around the sun. What a tremendous force the Earth must possess!

A few times each year, we marvel at the awesome power of typhoons. At the same time, we gape at how much greater the power of nature is than that of human beings. Where does this awesome power of nature come from? What is its source?

All the myriad things in this world have their own forms and colors. Truth makes each fruit ripen from its own seed and allows all other things around it to exist together in harmony. It naturally delivers adversity for the person who has transgressed and benefit for the person who has created good karma.

This is the wisdom and grace of Truth. It is the Truth Buddha that delivers such creative transformations and capabilities. In short, the unlimited gracious workings of Truth are its awesome power.

All sentient beings live within the grace of that awesome power. Yet, most are unaware of it. Because they are ignorant of the grace and power of Truth, average people and sentient beings may be blind to the grace they have received, in which case they may experience hardship due to their ingratitude.

If we awaken to Il-Won-Sang Truth and practice in the realm of Samādhi, where our mind is free from erratic states of mind and scattered thoughts, and we awaken also to the Gateway of Birth and Death that transcends Being and Nonbeing, we can gain the dharma power of those who have become one with Il-Won-Sang. We will then live our lives having achieved the unlimited and awesome power of Truth.

We humans cannot rely on our power alone. Our lives become far more powerful when we can draw from the power of the whole. It was once said that "we must at least draw upon the energy of the ridge between rice fields." This means that all things depend on one another no matter how insignificant or important they may seem individually.

If a family member is appointed to a high government post, that family is said to have cause for celebration. When there is a government official in your family, your influence improves, and you gain power.

In human society, "power" refers to things such as economic might and privileges. But when we awaken to the Truth and engage in true requital of grace, we gain the tremendous might of Truth. It could be said that the power of the buddha-bodhisattva is a potent force—like the power of Heaven and Earth.

Average people need to have solid collateral to borrow money from the bank. But when someone has solid credit, he can borrow a lot of money without necessarily having to put anything up for collateral.

Truth is the same way. To the practitioners who are utterly committed to requiting the Fourfold Grace and to upholding their vows with prayer, Truth confers the awesome might of its grace. How could it not do so, when they live a life of great faith, engage in the Threefold Practice appropriately, perform requital of grace, and make proper buddha offerings?

Awesome might is the grace afforded us by those around us: our parents, our Teachers (our teachers are our spiritual parents), and our fellow beings. For instance, I know of someone who is strangely blessed with innate virtue. Despite having no capital to speak of, this person always does well through the help of others. This is an example of "awesome power."

It is not only us humans who live in this world. There are also heavenly beings and asuras, and it is said that in some cases they help practitioners who are especially committed to their practice and their life of faith. That too could be described as a kind of awesome power.

When buddha-bodhisattvas establish the power of aspiration to help others and offer their prayers, the Dharmakāya Buddha, Fourfold Grace displays its wondrous and awesome power to aid them in these tasks. When such wondrous aid falls on average people, they will say that luck was with them because something they expected to fail, succeeded instead. Although there might have been an element of fortune involved, it was really the awesome power of the Fourfold Grace, of Heaven and Earth, parents, fellow beings and laws, that delivered the good fortune.

Beginning three years before the 1988 Seoul Olympic Games, Master Daesan delivered many dharma talks in which he spoke of "going beyond the walls of tribalism, beyond the walls of the state, beyond the walls of religion." He said that peace would only arrive once our world allowed freedom in those three areas. Strangely enough, the theme of the 1988 Olympics became "breaking down the walls."

"Going beyond the walls" and "breaking down the walls" are very similar in meaning, so it was quite astonishing when the theme of the Games was announced.

It is said that the person who engages in deep Truth practice possesses the power of Heaven, that is, possesses the power to deliver creative transformations of Truth, like those of Heaven itself.

A person who is elected president assumes total authority for the government. In the same way, one who becomes a presiding buddha for the age by engaging in profound practice acquires the remarkable power of Truth.

An instance of this remarkable power was evidenced when the nine senior disciples of Won Buddhism, having prayed with utmost sincerity and the spirit of "Sacrifice with no Regret," stamped their bare fingers on paper and produced seals of blood. But because sages must provide an example for sentient beings, they use the creative transformations and awesome power of nature rather than engage in supernatural miracles.

Persons who have engaged in mind practice and become one with Truth have a tremendous power to move people—they can command the minds of others as they wish. This is the awesome power of mercy. A buddha-bodhisattva is filled with the spirit of reverence for the Buddha—free from harmful thoughts, free from the selfish desire to serve oneself and primarily interested in knowing how to help others. The minds of those who meet the buddha-bodhisattva melt away—they become an embodiment of that unlimited influence.

During his long struggle with illness, Master Chŏngsan heard that some of his students were offering a special prayer for his recovery. "You do not have to say any more prayers," he said, "for I am someone known to the Dharma Realm, and the Dharma Realm knows my life and knows my death."

Could average people say that they are known to the Dharma Realm? Master Chŏngsan, who possessed the awesome power of Heaven and Earth was able to say that the Dharma Realm knew him.

Once we have become recognized by the Dharma Realm, what could we worry about? What should we fight tooth and nail to possess? Let us all practice with diligence so that each of us becomes recognized by the dharma realm and can wield that awesome power.

"... we attain the awesome power of Il-Won and become one with the nature of Il-Won."

Attaining the awesome power of and becoming one with the nature of Il-Won means that we awaken to the Dharmakāya Buddha, Il-Won Sang Truth that governs all the myriad things of the universe as well as the Dharma Realm of Empty Space, and that we live that Truth.

There is but one Il-Won-Sang Truth in this universe. It is not the case that God, Heaven, and The Way exist separately—there is only the one Truth. The one Truth we call "the Pure Dharmakāya Buddha."

When we clearly see Our true nature of the Dharmakāya Buddha (Truth Buddha) and when we model our bodies and minds wholeheartedly on its purity, we experience "the perfect Sambhogakāya Buddha (Bliss Buddha)." When we experience and come to possess Truth in this way, we are said to have become a buddha.

A person who has become a Sambhogakāya Buddha acquires its

wisdom and compassion. When that person interacts with sentient beings, that wisdom and compassion linger within their minds as the embodiment of the Nirāmaṇakāya Buddha (Manifestation Buddha). This means that their buddhahood—their true nature—has become deeply impressed in their characters as the standard for their lives. When we possess this Triple Buddha Body in ourselves, it is said that we have become one with the awesome power and nature of Il-Won-Sang Truth.

The beginning part of the Vow says that Il-Won is "the realm of Samādhi beyond words and speech." This refers to the state of Samādhi where there are no signifiers, no differentiation, and no time or space. The Vow also says that Il-Won is "the Gateway of Birth and Death that transcends Being and Nonbeing." When we can generate a mind that transcends all things, we can say that we have attained that awesome power and we have become one with the nature of Il-Won.

The Founding Master addressed the congregation at a meditation hall, "Who among you has completed a of ownership of the Dharma Realm of Empty Space?" The congregation was silent—no one replied. The Founding Master said, "Because all the buddhas and bodhisattvas of the three time-periods work hard to take possession of the formless and invisible Dharma Realm of Empty Space, they are able to own even the myriads of things in Heaven and Earth that possess form. Average people and sentient beings, on the contrary, are greedily attached to things that have form, yet they never manage to possess them. instead, they end up wasting their precious time. How can this not be deluded? Do not exhaust yourselves trying to possess only things that have form; work hard instead to take possession of the formless Dharma Realm of

Empty Space."

In "The Dharma of Timeless Zen" we are asked to learn The Way through practice that takes true emptiness as its substance and marvelous existence as its function. Once our practice of The Way matures so that we never part with our original mind, we become one with its substance and nature. The Founding Master said that we must transfer ownership of the Dharma Realm of Empty Space to ourselves. In other words, we must make the empty space that is Truth into something that is utterly ours.

When we buy or sell property, we usually make a donor payment. Once we pay the balance, the tittle of the property is transferred to our name. Only when the tittle is in our name does it become our property. In the same way, transferring registration of Il-Won-Sang Truth into our name requires the investment of tremendous amounts of mind, body, and matter.

Knowing that awakening to and becoming one with Il-Won-Sang Truth requires an investment, when we invest in a business, we should also invest in making Il-Won-Sang ours. Then both ventures will prosper even more.

When we speak of modeling ourselves wholeheartedly on Il-Won-Sang Truth, it means emulation. But before there is emulation, there has to be discovery—the discovery of a model worthy of emulation. It is important to listen to the experience of those who have already modeled themselves on Il-Won-Sang by means of practice. This will lead to a place of faith in teachers and in the study of the scriptures, which are accounts of such experiences.

Let us maintain faith in our teachers and diligently do as they instruct us. As we follow them, we will discover the footprints of Truth.

"Seeing our true nature" means the experiential understanding of the Realm of the Great, the realm of emptiness, and the realm of Nonbeing. Once we achieve that understanding, we are one with our ever-calm and ever-alert mind. This mind (the Realm of the Great, the realm of Emptiness, and the Realm of Nonbeing) is called the Truth that neither arises nor ceases. Awakening to this means understanding the jewel that lies within each of us.

Let us recognize this and make significant investments so that we can transfer that ownership to our name. Let us commit ourselves sincerely—investing our devotion, investing our time, and sometimes investing our wealth—so that we may awaken to the One Mind.

Once we engage deeply in mind practice, we awaken to the fact that the Truth of the karmic principle of cause and effect—in which we reap as we sow—is not at all separate from the principle of alternating predominance of yin and yang that accounts for changes in the universe. We will also awaken to the fact that the actions that are right or wrong, beneficial or harmful, are not separate from the principles of Great and Small, Being and Nonbeing. We will awaken with certitude to the fact that the principles of the mind are essentially the same as the workings of the universe. This is called the "Perfect and Right Enlightenment."

Based on this awakening to and understanding of all principles, we will engage in sincere and great dedication to attain the *Beyond the Household* Stage and the *Greatly Enlightened Tathāgata* Stage. We will then become one with the essence of the universe. We will enter Samādhi in Action and Samādhi at Rest, so that action and rest merge into one. In the *Diamond Sutra*, this is called "Nirvana without Residue." It is a state of unbroken Nirvana, of ultimate bliss in every time and at every place.

The Founding Master said that sentient beings suffer because their minds do not operate as they wish, which creates a hell within them. The sentient being's body becomes accustomed to functioning as it will because there is no-mind controlling it. As a result, a hell reigns in the sentient being's relationships and karmic ties.

Instead, the bodhisattva, knows the principles of the mind and trains accordingly, knows the body and trains its habits effectively, and addresses all affinities with the wisdom mind. If we practice in this way, we can turn the mind, the body, all karmic affinities, the world, and Heaven and Earth, into ultimate bliss, and we can become the masters of bliss ourselves.

This truly is becoming one with the awesome power and nature of Il-Won-Sang Truth.

CHAPTER 8

CONCLUSION OF
THE IL-WON-SANG VOW

We must live our lives following our Will—the will to become buddhas and benefit the world. Let us not live for the sake of pleasure. If we live for pleasure and enjoyment, we may enjoy ourselves for a time, but we will not know what to do when we encounter pain.

There is a deep joy that arises when we live following our Will—not just any ordinary will. Let us all adopt Truth as our home, adopt the actions of Truth as our actions, defeat Māra and bring it into submission. Let us make a firm vow to progress and receive great grace—It is important to know whether we do possess that kind of Will or we do not.

If we make a great vow here and now, there will be an early consecration ceremony for us in the realm of the gods. "That person is sure to be a buddha before long," they will say, "Let us hold the consecration now."

The gist of our vow could be described as an instruction to "live following our Will"—to "follow our will to become a buddha."

How many times do you recite the Il-Won-Sang Vow each day? If you do it ten times a day or more, then you are doing around five thousand recitations in a year. Some people are said to recite it twenty times in the morning and evening. For those of you who do so, I ask that you do it without thinking of the words for a few times, and then do it one or two times while focusing on the meaning.

To those who have not done it yet, I ask that you do ten to twenty recitations each day. If you recite it frequently, the grace of the sages will be with you. Those in the realm of the buddhas and bodhisattvas care for the person who frequently recites the scriptures of the Buddha.

There are a number of things that the Founding Master said frequently. Let me share some of them with you.

There was a Confucian scholar named Lee. One day, it was raining heavily, and he entered a temple to escape the downpour. Next to the temple, he saw written the words *The Flower Ornament Sutra*. That's a good name for a sutra, he thought to himself.

Sometime after that, he died. Once we die our vision becomes delusional, so that the world of insects or the furs of animals may seem more appealing than a human body, and a body may look like a house. So it was that the scholar Lee was about to enter "a nice house" (what looked like an appealing body), when someone suddenly struck his head with a wooden clapper and said, "Hey! What is a guy who learned *The Flower Ornament Sutra* doing heading for a dog house?" For he was above to enter the womb of a dog. At this, he is said to have revived with a start.

Those who recite the Buddha's teachings frequently are said to be assisted by the good gods and good asuras that exist to assist the Buddha. They guide the person who has followed the Buddha's teachings and recited them frequently, onto the proper path. They are said to ask, "Is it right that such a person should end up in a dog house?"

If we practice constantly toward the ten thousand spiritual cultivations, the ten thousand cultivations of wisdom, and the ten thousand cultivations of virtue, the ten billion spiritual cultivations, the ten billion cultivations of wisdom, and the ten billion cultivations of virtue, and the immeasurable spiritual cultivations, the immeasurable cultivations of wisdom, and the immeasurable cultivations of virtue, we will change the nameplate on our door—we will no longer be the sentient beings that we were before. Our nameplate will read "buddha-bodhisattva" instead.

Until that day, I hope that every one of you will practice with great dedication.

AFTERWORD FOR THE 2012 EDITION

This book on the Il-Won-Sang Vow has been compiled from recordings of lectures given over a nine-day period at the Tuesday retreats during my time as head of the Seoul District. The lectures were delivered so that all attending Won Buddhists, including myself, might inherit and practice the Founding Master's plan for compassionate action.

At times, the lectures lack systematic explanation, and at times I pass over things if I believe they refer to a situation that everyone already understands. For this reason, I have reviewed the text and added some information, but because it is structured around lecture content, there are some aspects that I find unsatisfactory for publication as a book. Still, I decided to publish it, hoping it would serve as an opportunity to help others understand the great teacher's will in some small degree. If the reader notifies me of any aspect of it that needs revision, I will humbly accept the suggestions and revise it accordingly.

I would like to extend my sincerest appreciation to the minister who worked hard to make the recordings and who provided, as well, revisions and supplementation for the publication of this book. I would also like to extend my sincerest appreciation to the ministers who worked on this publication.

The Author

ABOUT THE AUTHOR

Venerable Kyongsan (1940 -) is the Fifth Head Dharma Master of Won Buddhism.

He entered the Won Buddhist faith at the age of twenty, and graduated from the Department of Won-Buddhist Studies at Wonkwang University in 1968. He served as President of the Youngsan College of Zen Studies, Executive Director of Administration at the Won Buddhism Headquarters, and Director of the Jung-Do Retreat Center, before being inaugurated as the Fifth Head Dharma Master in 2006.

Ven. Kyongsan envisions a One World community of truth and unity. In devotion to this vision, he has dedicated himself to the ideals of his predecessor Ven. Daesan, the Third Head Dharma Master. Ven. Daesan's ideals, termed "Three Proposals for World Peace," comprise the undevelopment of moral discipline for cultivating the mind; the creation of a unified world market; and the establishment of a worldwide organization of United Religions.

The practice to realize Ven. Kyongsan's vision constitute: first, the Great Buddha Offering, second, the Embodiment of the Won Buddhist Dharma, third, the Universal Spreading of Grace, and fourth, the Sowing of Blessings for the Coming Centuries.

Ven. Kyongsan has written many books, including *The World of Lao-tzu, Herding the Ox of Our Mind, The Middle Way, The Shore of*

Freedom: Commentary on The Heart Sutra, The Functioning of a Buddha's Mind, and *Freedom from Transgressive Karma.*